Mary Ann Nowlan   49

THE KNOWLEDGE LIBRARY

HOW BIRDS BEHAVE

THE KNOWLEDGE LIBRARY

HOW BIRDS BEHAVE

By Neil Ardley

Illustrated by David Andrews

GROSSET & DUNLAP

Publishers · NEW YORK
A National General Company

Published in the United States of America by
Grosset & Dunlap, Inc. New York, N.Y.

FIRST PRINTING 1971
Copyright © 1969, 1971 by The Hamlyn Publishing Group, Ltd.
All Rights Reserved.
Adapted from the Grosset All-Color Guide: BIRD BEHAVIOR
Library of Congress Catalog Card Number: 77–154874
ISBN: 0–448–00367–8 (Trade Edition)
ISBN: 0–448–07261–0 (Library Edition)
Printed by Officine Grafiche Arnoldo Mondadori, Verona, Italy.

contents

Page

Birds Can Be Fascinating   6

Keeping Clean   10

Finding Food and Drink   16

Living Together   28

The Language of Birds   32

Setting about Breeding   36

Nesting and
Looking after the Young   52

Learning about Life   64

Migration   69

Index   74

BIRDS CAN BE FASCINATING

Apart from the icy regions of the North and South Poles and the summits of very high mountains, there is probably no place on earth that has never seen a bird.

Many of us have the opportunity of seeing birds every day, although probably only a few of the 8,600 different kinds of species may be observed. Birds influence our lives in various ways. We keep them as pets; we stalk them with binoculars and cameras – and hunt them with guns; we feed them in our parks and on our lawns – and eat their meat and eggs; and we may even wear their feathers for decorative effect.

Animals that move a lot are always more appealing than those that do not, and birds move in the most fascinating way of all – they fly. People, of course, can only dream of flying. When we watch birds gliding effortlessly through the air, we may secretly envy them, and perhaps that may explain why birds seem to be one of the most popular of all groups of animals.

Birds also interest us because of their dependence on vision, a dependence that we share ourselves.

Above: The Tawny Owl, like all owls, has huge eyes that enable it to hunt at night.

Left: All birds of prey, like these Brown Harrier Eagles, use their eyes to detect their potential victims from overhead heights before swooping down for the capture.

Right: Songbirds escaping from a cat. Such alert action often means the difference between life and death. Birds that are able to take wing as soon as they detect an enemy approaching will live and breed. But birds that react slowly will soon be caught. To be on the safe side, most birds will flee regardless of whether the approaching animal is friendly or unfriendly. But some birds, such as pigeons in public squares, learn to change their natural behavior when it is to their advantage.

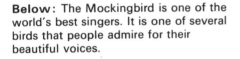

Below: The Mockingbird is one of the world's best singers. It is one of several birds that people admire for their beautiful voices.

Like humans, birds use their eyes to find out about the world around them, whereas most other animals rely primarily on their sense of smell to hunt their prey or identify their own kind. We have all seen our pet dogs or cats investigate something new by sniffing, which is not the way we would go about it! But birds use their eyesight to find food and to detect each other, as do humans. And like us, they act or behave in special ways toward each other. They themselves create colorful displays that are attractive and interesting. Birds also utilize sound in a meanihgful way. Their voices, ranging from the comical mimicry of parrots and mynah birds to the beautiful sweet song of the canary and the nightingale, can cause both amusement and delight.

These are some of the fascinating aspects of bird behavior. Also of much interest is the reason birds behave as they do.

BEHAVIOR FOR SURVIVAL

From the moment a bird hatches from its egg, its every action becomes vital to survival. It first needs warmth, food, and protection, which is usually derived from its parents, but it must act in a correct way to get them. When it leaves the nest, a bird must seek its own food and shelter, and keep itself clean. It must avoid enemies, and it will have to find a mate in order to breed. Its life will never be easy. Failure usually means death. A bird's survival will depend on how it behaves at critical moments.

Above: A small European songbird called the Great Titmouse is able to use its feet and bill in a remarkably efficient manner to acquire a morsel of food on the end of a piece of string. It pulls up about half the length of the string with its beak, and holds it in place with its feet. In this way, the food is raised high enough for the bird to take it in its bill. Such actions do not come automatically, but must be learned by the bird. Titmice can learn to use their bills and feet in ingenious ways, because this type of behavior comes naturally to them and suits their way of life. A canary, on the other hand, would find it difficult to learn such a trick because it does not normally use its bill and feet together to feed.

Many of a bird's actions have direct survival value. A bird eluding a pouncing cat is behaving that way to keep itself alive. With the same purpose, a bittern among the reeds will freeze into immobility at the close approach of an enemy, so that it will not be detected. Both kinds of behavior have evolved by *natural selection*; that is, the birds which survive are those that are best at survival behavior, and this survival ability is passed on to their offspring. Each of a bird's behavior patterns helps it to survive in some way or other. In most cases, birds are born with these behavior patterns. Sometimes, however, behavior is acquired through learning from experience.

KINDS OF BEHAVIOR

Birds constantly behave in many different ways, but their actions may be placed into two basic categories. One type of behavior keeps the bird itself alive and well and does not affect other birds very much. Such actions include flying, feeding and cleaning, which are called *maintenance activities*. The other type of behavior has to do with a bird's relationship toward other birds – how it "talks" or makes another bird respond in some way. These *social activities* are called *displays*. Behaving in an accepted way toward others is an important rule where birds live together in large groups, just as human beings have developed customs and laws that make living together possible.

Displays may consist of set movements carried out like rituals, or of various unusual postures. They may look absurd, but each has an exact meaning to the birds involved.

Ethologists, or scientists who study behavior, must look attentively at the situations in which displays occur. A display by a male bird on a chosen nesting site means it is ready to mate; but chiefly the bird is warning other males to keep away from the territory which will provide food for its family.

THE SIGNAL TO ATTACK

Some kinds of actions are caused by signals. The European Robin is an aggressive bird when it has territory to defend, and will attack any strange robins entering its territory. If so much as a bunch of red feathers were to be placed within that territory, the robin would be likely to attack the feathers as savagely as any rival. The mere sight of the strange robin's red breast acts as an attacking "signal" to the first robin, and so he attacks. The American Robin, a different species of bird, is also quite aggressive in defending its territory. The brightly colored chests of the males not only serve to attract females, but also warn off competitors.

LEARNING TO BEHAVE

Many of a bird's actions are inherited and instinctive. Young birds can fly as soon as they leave their nests. They do not always fly well right away, however, so they often have to "practice" flying before they become perfect. Certain behavior must be learned: finding the best place to roost; knowing what is good to eat and what isn't, and where to find food; learning which birds to avoid and which to harass – these are kinds of behavior that a bird can only learn from experience. Learning is important for birds, but not nearly as crucial as it is in human behavior.

Below: Young swallows can fly as soon as they leave the nest, and so they obviously do not have to learn the basic movements. But their flying ability improves with experience as they get older.

KEEPING CLEAN

Washing and bathing may sometimes seem to us to be a chore, but imagine how much worse it would be if you were a bird and covered with thousands of feathers! Even a bird the size of a sparrow has between two and three thousand feathers to deal with, all of them important. They trap a layer of air next to the skin which helps to keep the birds warm and, in water birds, to float. They enable the bird to fly, and their color patterns serve as social signals. Keeping feathers clean and in working order is therefore essential to a bird's well being.

It doesn't take long for plumage to become soiled and to need cleaning. Feathers get dirty quickly from pollen, dust and mud. Also parasites such as fleas and lice chew on the feathers and suck the bird's blood.

TAKING A BATH

Most birds bathe regularly. If they are stopped from doing so in captivity, they become quite unhappy and will jump into any available water as soon as they are released. The liquid helps to remove dirt from the feathers, and also facilitates preening the feathers after bathing.

Several kinds of birds like to bathe together. Seeing one bathing will make others want to join in as well. Robins will often crowd into the water together and splash around and really seem to be enjoying themselves. Thus the urge to bathe, like laughing among humans, can be "catching," and this helps to keep a flock together. Staying together in groups increases the chances of survival for many bird species.

Above: A goldfinch washes itself by first tipping its body forward into some water, thrashing its bill about, and flicking its wings up and down (top). Then it settles back on its tail and moves its wings to and fro across its back in a "scissoring" motion. Water is thus splashed over the bird's feathers (bottom). The goldfinch performs the two operations alternately, so that it rocks back and forth in the water.

Left: A group of Bronze-winged Manakins rest flank-to-flank and preen each other. Birds that sit together like this are called *contact* species because they are often in contact.

Left: A kingfisher washes itself by plunging into the water from the air. This is one of the easiest methods of getting the feathers wet before the bird sets about preening. Birds that spend prolonged periods in flight (these include swifts, terns and drongos) wash by this technique. The plunge probably helps to dislodge some dirt from the feathers. Preening with the beak serves to recondition the feathers for flying, and to remove parasites, such as fleas and mites, from the plumage.

Methods of bathing vary. Water birds have only to dip down below the surface, sometimes turning a somersault, to get wet all over. They then rub their heads along their sides and wings. Most land birds bathe by standing in shallow pools of water, spreading their feathers to let the water penetrate, and some jump in and out of the water, over and over again. Some birds, especially larks, bathe in the rain. Parrots and hornbills spread out their feathers to get wet, whereas we put up umbrellas to stay dry! Grouse, pheasants and turkeys do not bathe in water at all, but prefer dust baths to clean themselves.

Left: As shown by this thrush, birds become dirty and dishevelled when they do not preen properly.

PREENING

A bath in water is not sufficient to get the plumage into perfect condition again. In much the same way that humans use creams and lotions to condition their skin, birds use a special oil to restore their feathers. This oil is a waxy substance contained in an oil gland beneath some feathers on the bird's back. After shaking and fluttering its wings to get rid of the water left from bathing, the bird turns its head, wipes its beak to clean it, and takes some oil from

Above: Male and female Oriental White-eyes preen each other.

Above: A male Mallard obtains oil from its oil gland for preening. The gland is usually covered by overlapping feathers. An oil gland is especially important to water birds such as ducks, because oil helps to make the feathers repel water. If the oil gland is removed, the bird is crippled for swimming.

Left: House Sparrows take dust baths to clean themselves! They scratch away hollows in the soil and then sift dust through their feathers, thus removing fleas and mites.

Above: A female Cuban Finch preens a male, which raises its feathers to invite preening.

Right: A Common Jay "anting." Anting is an unorthodox method of cleaning, adopted by at least 160 kinds of birds. The jay sits with its feathers fluffed out over some ants, and allows them to stream over its body. The ants squirt formic acid, which probably acts as an insecticide to kill parasites.

the gland. It then smears the oil over the feathers, a process known as *preening*. The wing feathers come first, because the bird must restore its full powers of flight as soon as possible. Then the rest of the body is preened. Some finches take as long as twenty minutes to preen.

Oiling is especially important to water birds because it helps to waterproof the feathers. When water "rolls off a duck's back," it is the oil on the duck's feathers that causes this to happen.

Scientists have shown that in sunshine, this oil produces vitamin D. When this vitamin is absorbed

into the body, it helps prevent a bone disease called rickets. Sometimes the oil is colored and used like cosmetics! Some gulls and terns apply rose-colored oil to their breasts in the breeding season, and the yellow oil of the great hornbill is smeared on its wings.

A few birds do not have an oil gland. These are ostriches, emus, cassowaries, frogmouths and bustards, among the land birds, and, oddly enough, those great fishermen, the cormorants.

Several kinds of birds like to preen each other, as monkeys do. One bird fusses with the feathers of the bird sitting next to it, often in answer to a special preening invitation, which may consist of a ruffling of feathers, or a facing away so that the neck is presented conspicuously. This social preening, or *allopreening*, becomes particularly useful for cleaning hard-to-get-at places like the head region. Of the 155 living families of birds, 38 families, including such diverse groups as penguins, and crows, show this behavior.

HEAD SCRATCHING

A bird's head obviously cannot be preened with its own bill. If a bird does not have a companion to do it for him, then he has to scratch with his claws instead. Most birds scratch *directly*, by bringing the leg up under the wing. But some birds scratch *indirectly*, with the leg brought up over the wing. Most perching birds – including turacos, swifts, hummingbirds, Hoopoes, oyster-catchers, avocets and stilts – scratch in this manner. Some birds, such as wood warblers and parrots, are able to use both methods.

Scratching is very important to birds that fish for food, such as herons. By spending so much time in or near water, their feathers become soiled with slime. The usual cleaning methods are of little use. Herons, however, have patches of downy feathers that produce a fine powder. They "comb" this powder over their feathers with their claws, and it soaks up the slime.

Above: A Starling uses its bill to apply some ants to its feathers. It is theorized that anting may help to keep the feathers in good condition, it may kill parasites such as fleas and mites, it may relieve itching, or it may just feel pleasant.

Left: A male Hyacinth Macaw cleans its head by scratching with its leg brought up directly.

Above: A Red Avadavat (a small grassfinch of India) preens itself after bathing. It first wipes its beak clean (1), and then takes oil from its oil gland (2). The oil is smeared over the bill and then transferred to the feathers. The avadavat draws its primary wing feathers through its bill to preen them (3), but other wing feathers are preened by twisting the head backward (4). Turning the neck is sufficient for getting at the rump feathers (5), but the tail has to be twisted around for the vent to be cleaned (6). The wing is spread to preen underwing feathers (7). The entire procedure takes about ten minutes.

Left: A male Bullfinch scratches indirectly — it brings one leg over its lowered wing.

FINDING FOOD AND DRINK

Eating and drinking are as important to birds as they are to all living things, including ourselves. But, in some ways, eating and drinking are even more important to a bird than to a human. As they fly, birds use up immense amounts of energy to keep their wings flapping, and must therefore eat large quantities of food just to keep going. Hummingbirds, which hover in the air by moving their wings back and forth very rapidly, burn up amazing quantities of energy. If a man worked at the same rate as the hummingbird, he would have to eat as much as twice his own weight in food every day to get the required energy! And he would have to drink almost his own weight in water every hour just to keep cool!

Few birds use as much energy as hummingbirds, but life for all birds is a constant search for food, especially in winter. Titmice have to find a morsel of food every $2\frac{1}{2}$ seconds for nine-tenths of the day during the winter. Wood Pigeons search for food for 95 per cent of the daylight hours. If these birds did not work so hard at finding food, they would starve.

Birds eat all kinds of food, from the tiny algae (one-celled plants) that flamingos take from the salt water of the East African lakes where they live, to the monkeys that are the favorite dish of certain

Above: Greenfinches drink by lowering their heads into a pool and taking up some water in their beaks. Then they raise their heads and tip the water back down their throats, just like a person gargling. Most birds drink in this manner.

Left: A jay is startled by a moth suddenly opening its brightly spotted wings. The bird flies away and the moth is saved. Because they are the favorite prey for many birds, insects have developed numerous ways of avoiding capture. This moth resembles the bark of a tree when its wings are folded, and any birds looking for food will probably miss it if it is resting on a tree. But if its wings are spread open, they reveal two strange eye-spots. These spots look so much like eyes that the bird possibly thinks it is facing a much larger animal than the moth. Some insects that have a bad taste also have bright patterns. A bird, once having eaten such an unsavory morsel, learns to associate the bright color with the bad taste. From then on, the bird will not touch insects marked in this way.

Right: This Ring Dove drinks in a way unique among birds. It puts its beak into a pool or a puddle and sucks water up in on long draught, like a horse. Sand grouse and some grass-finches that live in deserts also suck up water. In deserts, this method of drinking prevents any waste.

eagles in the Philippines. Many birds turn over leaves, dig into the soil, probe into the bark and trunks of trees – in fact, do almost anything – to find tasty insects. Some birds even follow large animals which stir up insects as they move around. Birds of prey, like many eagles, hawks, and owls, live on small mammals such as mice and rabbits, snakes, lizards, some of the larger insects, and other birds. Sea birds and water birds catch fish, crabs and water snails. Many other kinds of birds prefer plants to animals. Perching birds, like the finches, eat nuts and seeds; hummingbirds and sunbirds live on the

Right: The kinds of seeds that a bird eats depends on the size and strength of its beak. Birds with light bills will eat large amounts of small seeds that they can open quickly, rather than struggle to open large seeds. The Linnet, which has a light and delicate bill, eats large amounts of small seeds such as millet (top). The Greenfinch has a strong bill and eats small amounts of large seeds, such as sunflower seeds (center). The Chaffinch prefers medium-sized seeds such as hemp seeds, as its bill is not strong enough to handle large seeds (bottom).

Above: The Skimmer's beak (1) acts like a trap. The beak is opened and the lower mandible (jaw) slices through the water. When it touches something to eat, down comes the top mandible like a mousetrap.
The Flamingo (2) can strain plankton from the water with special fringes in its sieve-like bill. Both the Hawaiian Honeycreeper (3) and the Puff-legs Hummingbird (4) have long, thin beaks to probe down into flowers to reach the nectar.

nectar of flowering plants. It is easier to get food from plants than to eat animals, as animals will either try to flee or fight back. Some animal-eating birds surmount this difficulty by eating carrion – dead carcasses of animals.

Vultures, for instance, are notorious for eating carrion. On occasion, birds will steal food from one another, as when the Bald Eagle lays an ambush for Ospreys returning with the fish they have caught. The eagle, the stronger bird, is able to attack an Osprey in midair and cause it to drop its fish. It then dives down and catches the fish before it reaches the ground or water below. Along the Atlantic coast of the United States, Laughing Gulls rush brown pelicans and steal some of the fish that the pelicans have caught in their pouch-like bills.

DRINKING

Obtaining water in some way is essential to all birds in order to replace the moisture that is lost from their bodies. In the Antarctic, penguins acquire water by eating snow, and elsewhere birds drink in several other ways. Birds that spend most of their time in the air will swoop down to a lake or stream and scoop up water in their beaks. Other birds prefer to drink on the ground, standing by the water and lowering their

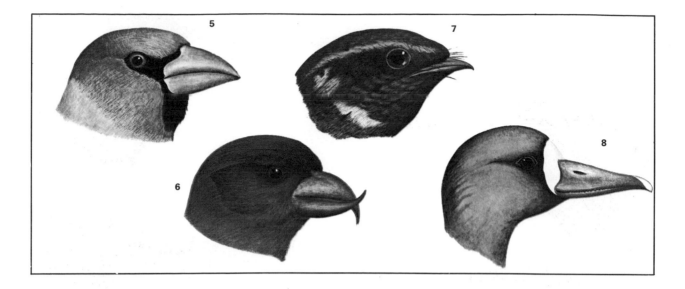

Above: Hawfinches (5) and Crossbills (6) have large, strong beaks for cracking open seeds. The Hawfinch can even open a cherry stone. The Nightjar (7) lives on insects. Its weak bill opens wide and the bristles around it help to catch insects. Geese, such as the White-fronted Goose (8), have bills with saw-like edges to crop grass.

heads to drink. A few birds, such as pigeons, suck up the water in much the same way as we drink through a straw. But most birds simply take some water in their bills, tip their heads back, and let it run down their throats.

Birds eat instinctively from the time they are born. Many of them seem to have a built-in set of directions that help them find the right food. But they may also have to learn where the best food is found, and catching it successfully often takes a good deal of practice. Drinking, too, does not always seem to be instinctive, and birds may have to learn to recognize water and to drink it. Some types of food contain more water than others. A bird living on insects, for instance, gets more water in its food than a bird that lives on seeds.

BEAKS, BEAKS, BEAKS

Birds have a variety of beaks or bills, ranging from the large colorful jaws of the toucan and strange paddles of the spoonbill to the elegant tweezers of some hummingbirds and the tiny forceps of the sparrow. But however strange-looking, each bird's beak is the appropriate shape and size to enable its owner to get the food it needs.

Birds with small beaks, such as members of the thrush family, use their beaks to grasp food before swallowing it. They catch insects, particularly grubs and larvae, and worms in their beaks, and they also eat plants, especially fruit. Fruit-eating birds, such as robins, will gorge themselves on overripe cherries and may even become slightly intoxicated!

Above: Most birds of prey have hooked beaks to tear at their prey, but the rare Everglade Kite uses its beak to get water snails out of their shells.

1

2

3

4

Above: The Huia is an extinct bird of New Zealand. The male Huia (1) and female Huia (2) had different beaks and so could eat different kinds of food. The male uncovered insects, while the female probed holes for them. The Great Spotted Woodpecker (3) has a beak like a chisel for uncovering insects that bore holes into wood. The Red-breasted Merganser (4) has a beak with saw-tooth edges to grip the slippery fish that it captures.

Many birds have long, thin bills which they use as probes, chisels or spears. Hummingbirds have fine, pointed bills with which they seek out the nectar in flowers. And wading birds, such as herons, often probe about under water looking for fish, frogs and other water creatures on the bottom. A woodpecker has a chisel-like beak to gouge away the bark of a tree and dig into the wood in search of wood-boring insects. Once the woodpecker discovers its victims, it catches them by darting its long tongue down the holes they have bored. Oyster-catchers use their long, thin beaks as chisels to attack partly open oyster shells and get at the molluscs inside. Kingfishers (and several other water birds) use their sharp beaks as spears to pierce and hold fish.

Several birds have very unusual beaks. The pelican can dive and scoop up several fish at once in its roomy, pouch-like bill. But it also traps water that has to drain away before the fish are swallowed, and a pelican's beak acts as a "strainer" to do this.

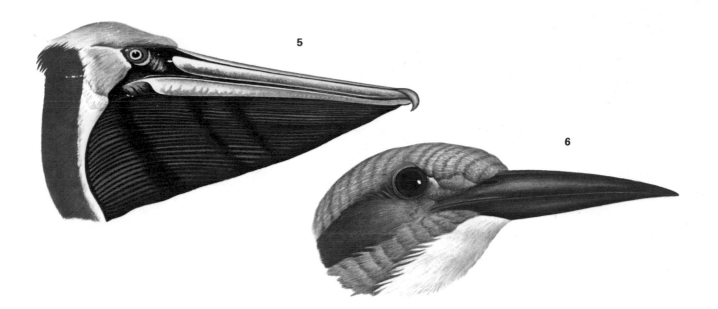

5

6

Some fish-eating birds, such as the Red-breasted Merganser, have bills with saw-toothed edges to help grip their slippery victims. The Skimmer has an unusual way of feeding. It flies over the water with its large bill open wide and one mandible, or jaw, just under the surface. By plowing through the water in this manner, it can scoop up fish in its beak. The flamingo has one of the most extraordinary beaks of all. This elegant pink bird stands on thin, stilt-like legs at the edges of lakes, poking in the mud at the bottom. Its curved bill and its huge tongue have fringes that act like sieves to strain out mud and water, leaving only minute plants and animals. In fact, the flamingo cannot swallow any large pieces of food at all because its tongue is in the way!

Many birds use their beaks as special tools for preparing food. Seed-eating birds use their beaks to crack open seed kernels to obtain the food inside. Many of them have strong bills that can open large seeds. The Crossbill is a seed-eater with a bill that looks like two crossed hooks which enables it to get the seeds out of evergreen cones before they have dried up and opened. Birds of prey use their hooked beaks to tear a victim to pieces before eating it.

Beaks may have other uses besides feeding. Parrots use their strong, curved beaks not only to crack open seeds and bite chunks out of fruits, but also to clamber about, as in a cage. Many birds have beaks with colorful markings that serve to identify the sex or species of the bird. The markings are also helpful in feeding the young, and this will be explained later.

Above: The Brown Pelican (5) traps fish inside its pouch-like bill, but the Common Kingfisher (6) has a pointed beak with which to spear fish.

Below: The Blue Titmouse often holds pieces of food in its feet. Titmice will also pull branches toward them to help them get at some food. These birds are very deft at using their feet. By using its feet and bill together, a titmouse can pull up the food as shown on pages 8 and 9. Titmice can be tamed to eat from the hand, and are sometimes trained to perform clever tricks.

Left: The Purple Gallinule can use its feet to pick up pieces of food. This is an unusual way for a bird to feed, for most birds simply grasp their food in their beaks. The Purple Gallinule is a brightly-colored water bird of the Americas. It lives in marshes as far north as the southern United States and as far south as Uruguay and northern Argentina. It is just over 12 inches long. The Gallinule's feet are not webbed, but its toes are very long and prevent it from sinking into the masses of water plants among which it lives. The toes have flexible joints that permit the grasping of pieces of food. Gallinules make nests of floating vegetation.

FEEDING WITH FEET AND CLAWS

Several birds use their feet as well as their beaks in their search for food. A bird just walking through the grass or bushes will stir up insects that it can then catch. Some herons and other waders will stamp about in shallow water for the same reason.

A bird of prey will first use its sharp claws or talons to strike its victim; it will then utilize its talons as meat hooks to hold the prey while its sharp beak tears the victim apart. Vultures are birds of prey, but they feed mainly on dead animals and so have no need to kill or hold their food. As a result, vultures have comparatively weak feet. But some birds are very dexterous in using their feet, such as parrots, owls and titmice. Titmice can use their feet to pull up a bit of food at the end of a length of string, in order to eat. (See pages 8 and 9.)

Right: The Short-billed Woodpecker Finch of the Galapagos Islands in the Pacific Ocean uses a spine from a cactus plant. If the insects it wants are in a deep hole or a crevice and out of reach, it takes a sharp cactus spine or small twig in its beak and probes down inside the hole or crevice. When the insect runs out, the Woodpecker Finch drops the spine and snaps up the insect in its beak. This tool-using ability, which is very rare in birds, is mostly instinctive. However, the bird learns to use the spine or twig more efficiently with practice. The Woodpecker Finch belongs to a group of 14 species of finches called Darwin's finches, which are found only on the Galapagos Islands. Darwin's study of how the differences among these closely related finches could have come about, led to his famous theory of the evolution of species over the course of time.

Right: An Egyptian Vulture drops a stone upon an ostrich egg to crack it open so that it can eat the contents. This is another example of a bird that can manipulate a tool to get something it wants. The Egyptian Vulture first chooses a heavy stone and picks it up in its beak. Then it walks over to the egg, raises itself on its toes, and lets go of the stone. Young birds do this instinctively as soon as they see an ostrich egg, but until they have had some practice, they often miss the egg and drop the stone to one side. This shows that part of the behavior is inborn in that the bird knows what to do, but part is learned in that the bird must practice to acquire good aim.

USING TOOLS

A few species of birds use other objects as tools to get at their food, although this is unusual and rare. The best known tool-using bird is the Short-billed Woodpecker Finch from the Galapagos Islands. This bird eats insects, but it catches them as follows: it breaks off a sharp spine from a cactus, or a small twig from a tree, and holds it in its beak. It then uses this "tool" for probing down holes and into crevices in trees and other places where insects might be. When the insects crawl out, the finch drops the spine or twig and gobbles them up.

Using a tool helps a bird to obtain extra food. The Egyptian Vulture uses large stones to crack open ostrich eggs. When a vulture finds an egg, it looks around for a heavy stone and picks one up

Right: A Blackbird looks on as a European Song Thrush breaks open a snail shell on a stone to get at the tasty snail inside. There are several birds that use the hard ground as an anvil against which they break hard-to-open food items. Some get their food out of hard shells by dropping the shells from the air onto rocks. Gulls often drop crabs or sea shells to break them open. The Lammergeyer, or Bearded Vulture, is particularly fond of eating bones. It carries large bones aloft in its talons and drops them onto special dropping areas. The bones crack open and the bird can get at the marrow inside.

in its beak. It walks over to the egg, stands over it on tiptoe, and drops the stone. The egg breaks, and the bird can then get at the rich yolk inside the egg. In Europe, the Song Thrush also uses rocks and stones to open snail shells, but in a different way: it takes a snail in its bill and smashes the shell against a hard rock. Other birds behave in a similar way. Gulls often drop crabs and sea shells from the air to crack them open and get at the soft insides. A graceful vulture bird called the Lammergeyer flies over specific land areas where it drops and cracks open bones, and tortoises.

Nuthatches and Great Spotted Woodpeckers have a special technique with hard nuts. They ram a nut into a gap in the bark of a tree or a crevice which they have chiseled out with their beaks. The crevice holds the nut tight, as in a vice, and the bird can then split it open with hammer-like blows of its beak.

Some Bowerbirds use tools in ways other than for feeding. They adorn their bowers with pigments from plants, using wads of bark or pads of leaves as brushes. Bowerbirds are shown on pages 50 and 51.

ARE BIRDS INTELLIGENT?

The fact that some birds know how to use a tool to get food might seem to indicate that these birds are intelligent in the human sense of the word. But their behavior is mainly instinctive, and the bird is acting without really thinking about it. Yet learning does play a role. Young birds do not always use a cactus spine or drop a stone in the most effective way and frequently miss getting their food. With acquired experience, however, they use their instinctive ability to better advantage.

There have been observations of bird behavior which suggest that some birds do use a certain amount of reasoning or intelligence to get food. A Green Heron was seen placing pieces of bread into a pond, thus managing to attract fish to the surface. The heron drove away any birds that were attracted to the bread, but ate the fish that nibbled the "bait." Then it saw some more fish swimming a few feet away, picked up other pieces of bread, and took those over for fresh "bait." This behavior is no different from that of a human fisherman, and it seemed that the heron knew what it was doing.

In Finland, during the winter, men fish by chopping holes in the ice that covers ponds and

Above: A Gray Jay stores seeds, such as acorns, and pieces of meat in a tree, sticking the food into its hiding place with its own saliva. The jay has special enlarged saliva glands to help it store food in this way. It fills its beak and throat with the food, then flies into the woods to hide it all away. Most birds that store food hide it beneath the ground. But the Gray Jay lives where deep snow covers the ground in winter, and so must store its food somewhere above the ground. Even if the food tree becomes covered with snow, the jay can usually remember where it is and will find it again without difficulty.

lakes, and dropping baited lines. A crow once dis-covered how to pull in lines by using its bill and walk-ing away from the hole. It would also lay down the line and dart back to stop that part of the line that had started to slip. It eventually drew up the length of the line until it got the fish at the end. Scientists have experimented with birds of the crow family and found that they are capable of solving difficult problems or puzzles. In the wild they will look for new sources of food if one supply runs out. Most other less-intelligent birds would not look elsewhere —and the chances are that they would starve.

STORING FOOD

Many birds starve to death in the winter when food is scarce, and many more would go hungry if it weren't for the breadcrumbs and other food that people put out for them. Certain birds, however, store food during the summer and autumn when it is plentiful and live off their hoards during the winter. Shrikes, for example, prepare larders of food by impaling beetles, lizards and nestling birds on thorns; although these birds migrate for the winter and do not need to store such food for long. For birds that do not migrate, however, the storing of food is essential for survival, and some species are extremely adept at hoarding. Acorn Woodpeckers, which live

Right: The Thick-billed Nutcracker finds a hidden store of hazel nuts that it has buried beneath the snow. This nutcracker lives in Scandinavia, where the winters are very cold. During the autumn, when hazel nuts ripen in the low-lands, the nutcrackers fly about, filling their throat pouches with them. The birds then fly off to higher ground three or four miles away, and bury their mouthfuls of nuts in holes in the ground. When winter comes, the nutcrackers can subsist off their food stores under the snow. Bird watchers in Sweden once kept watch on 351 nut stores through-out the winter. Although the snow was 20 inches deep, the birds ventured to nearly nine out of ten stores. Possibly the birds locate the nuts by remembering landmarks, such as trees or buildings. The nut stores often last into the spring, when the newly hatched young are fed with nuts stored the previous autumn! The one nut in ten that is missed may eventually grow into a tree. These birds thus help to spread the forest.

in small communities, bore holes in trees and can store as many as 50,000 acorns in each tree. Birds of the crow family are also good hoarders. In an oak wood in England, about 30 Common Jays were observed one October burying some 200,000 acorns! Although the birds are good at finding most of these acorns later, even under several inches of snow, a few are generally left over. This forgetfulness actually does Nature a favor by helping the growth of forests, especially at higher altitudes where acorns would not naturally be distributed. Some birds will simply work over an area very thoroughly to uncover their stores, but others use landmarks, such as trees or buildings, to help pinpoint a "hidden treasure."

FEEDING PARTNERSHIPS

Many people help keep birds alive by giving them food all year. But birds also benefit from people in ways other than being deliberately given handouts. European titmice often perch on milk bottles and peck through the foil tops to get to the milk inside.

A robin may swoop down and linger near a gardener turning over some soil, ready to pounce upon any worms that are dug up. At sea, gulls fly steadily behind a moving ship, awaiting any food leftovers which may be tossed overboard. Birds also form partnerships with animals, since by associating with them they can find food more readily than by fending for themselves. Cattle egrets often live

Right: Cattle Egrets live with oxen. These birds, also called Buff-backed Herons, live in most parts of the world. But wherever they live, they are always to be seen in the company of cattle. They feed on the insects and reptiles stirred up by browsing cattle, and can often be seen perching on the backs of their hosts. Zoologists have discovered that Cattle Egrets get more to eat in this way than if they were required to hunt their prey by themselves. Although they may seem to be clever birds, their behavior is instinctive and is not learned from others.

Opposite page: A European Robin grabs a wriggling worm brought up from under the earth by a man digging. Several species of birds often watch men digging and rush in to snatch the exposed worms. This is an example of a bird living in partnership with man in order to obtain food. Birds often realize that people will provide them with food, and come to live near them. Gulls follow ships, ready to swoop down and gobble up any food leftovers thrown overboard by the crew. Partnerships with people can make life easier for birds. They need do little more than just wait to be fed.

with herds of cattle, eating the insects and reptiles that the cattle disturb as they feed. Ptarmigans stay near caribou for the same reason, and gulls in Alaska pick up whatever may remain of salmon that the brown bears catch and eat.

Frequently in these feeding relationships the bird's behavior is also of benefit to the animal which provides the food. In Africa, oxpeckers live with oxen, rhinos and giraffes, sitting on their backs and eating small ticks and flies that infest their hosts' bodies. By this arrangement, the birds obtain food and the planteaters are rid of troublesome pests.

One of the more convenient "partnerships" is formed by the honey guide, a small forest bird of Africa and Asia. The African species, especially the Greater Honey Guide, hungers after the beeswax found in honeycombs in bees' nests. The honey guide cannot open a bees' nest to get at the wax, so it first attracts the attention of an animal, such as a honey badger or a bear, or even a human, and leads the way to the nest. The animal or man takes the honey and the honey guide has its fill of beeswax.

LIVING TOGETHER

The proverb, "Birds of a feather flock together," is true of numerous birds. Most birds, like humans, are socially inclined and prefer to live in each other's company. One needs only to look around parks and telephone wires during the winter to see great flocks of starlings roosting. Other birds, however, such as shrikes and most birds of prey, are solitary birds and stay in isolation for most of the year. All birds have to come together to breed, of course, and the breeding season is the only time when many solitary birds meet, either in groups or pairs.

Apart from the instinct for breeding, why is it that most birds "flock together?" And why is it that other birds do not? Consider the two major problems that birds must constantly face: (1) avoiding enemies and (2) getting food. Birds that live in flocks are less likely to be harassed by an enemy, because an intruder will immediately cause the flock to sound an alarm, and several birds can work together to drive the attacker away.

A solitary bird, while having none of these advantages, may have plumage that tends to blend in with the surrounding landscape. This camouflage helps keep the bird from attracting attention. The Rock Ptarmigan can even change its plumage to suit the season. In summer it is brownish, in autumn it becomes gray, and in winter it turns white! In this way, it always assumes the color of the rocky tundra in the northern lands it inhabits. It matches the low plants of summer, the bare rock of autumn, and the snows of winter.

The kind of food eaten also has to do with whether or not a particular bird is social or solitary. If an abundance of food can be found within a small area, such as berries on a tree, then the birds that eat the berries will flock together. One tree can provide enough food for an entire flock, and if the birds can eat without interfering with one another, then they are apt to stay together in the safety of numbers. Solitary birds, however, mostly depend on their stealth, speed and skill to get food. If they hunted in a group, they would disturb each other's prey and none of them would catch anything. But there are exceptions: insect-eaters, for example, may work together in seeking food. One bird will flush out insects for the others to catch.

Left: A group of Common Starlings, resting on a branch, space themselves out about four inches apart. Most social birds sit in rows with each bird just far enough from its neighbor so that one can jab at another if it feels annoyed. If they come closer one bird will threaten or avoid the other. Common Starlings have a beautiful blue-green sheen, and in autumn their feathers grow the striking white tips shown here. They are social birds and often live together in large groups. Starlings come in huge flocks to live in cities during the winter, and will take up residence on ledges of buildings and bridge girders. They can be a nuisance there, and are difficult to remove.

KEEPING ONE'S DISTANCE

Some birds sit in huddles, pressed closely together. Since most of these birds live in the tropics, huddling for warmth is not a factor. They simply enjoy the close contact. But in colder parts of the world, many birds do huddle for warmth. Wrens, tree creepers, titmices and swifts sometimes cluster together at night. The emperor penguins of the icy Antarctic huddle together when the weather is especially cold and windy. In this way, they can minimize the amount

Right: Skylarks do not always live together in flocks and, in fact, prefer to be on their own for much of the time. Many birds are solitary birds. For protection, these birds have plumage that matches in color the grassy plains and treeless fields in which they live, and they walk and run along the ground instead of hopping. Their light brown plumage acts as camouflage and protects them from their enemies. It is possible to get quite close to a Skylark on the ground without seeing the bird. Nevertheless, it will have seen you, and will suddenly fly up into the air, singing sweetly. Skylarks live in Europe, Asia and North Africa. They have been introduced successfully to New Zealand, Hawaii and Vancouver Island in Canada.

Right: A flock of Bohemian Waxwings may strip a bush of all of its berries before flying on to find another bush. Waxwings live together in large flocks. They migrate and stay together during the winter, and they also live in groups when they are breeding. Waxwings like to eat fruit and berries, particularly cherries and cedar and juniper berries. Flocks of waxwings wander from place to place in search of fruit, often moving from one area to another as the fruit becomes ripe. Species of waxwings live in Europe, Asia and North America.

of body heat lost by about one-fifth, and conserve the valuable reserves of fat that they have stored up within themselves.

Most social birds like to sit at a distance from one another. This distance varies from species to species. Generally, individual birds keep just far enough away from each other to be out of range of their neighbors' beaks. If one bird gets too near another, then a threatening jab or similar gesture signals an unmistakable warning.

Left: When birds band together to get food, each one has a specific rank and must await its designated turn to feed. The sequence for feeding is called a *pecking order.* These four birds have found some crumbs put out for them in the snow. The large, dominant Blue Jay (1) eats first, then the Starling (2). Next come the smaller birds, with the Purple Finch (3) dominating the Black-capped Chickadee (4). Although the pecking order is established by fighting, once established it helps to prevent any squabbling over the food because each bird knows its place and does not have to battle all over again to maintain its position.

Right: Two male Mandarin Ducks and a female go through the motions of drinking as a greeting ceremony to each other. This ceremony occurs among friendly ducks, and is common to many wild fowl. When birds live together in groups, such rituals are necessary to keep the birds peaceful. Humans behave in a similar way. We often shake hands with strangers to show good intentions and a friendly spirit. Sharing food and drink also helps people to talk and be friendly with one another. Birds that live in groups often behave in the same way at the same time, especially when they must deal with marauding enemies and find food. Mandarin Ducks live in the wild in Eastern Asia and Japan. They are a favorite with people who keep ducks, and can be seen in captivity in many parts of the world.

THE PECKING ORDER

We say that "the early bird gets the worm," but it would be more accurate to say "the strongest" or "the most aggressive" bird. This bird can bully the rest of the flock to get the best perches, the choicest food and the most desirable mates for itself. This principle extends to the "lower echelons" of the flock: each member gives way to a more dominant bird, but wins out over a less aggressive bird. The order of positions within a group is called the *pecking order*. Each bird acts in accordance with its prescribed rank and need not fight to keep it. Being the last in a pecking order is not always pleasant. When food is scarce, these timid birds will have little chance of eating. They would stand a better chance of surviving by leaving the flock and hunting for food on their own.

Birds of different species may sometimes seek food together, and a pecking order will thus come into being in such a mixed group as well as in a flock of the same species.

BEHAVING ALIKE

If you observe a flock of birds, you will see that most of the birds are behaving in the same way at the same time, whether they are bathing, resting, feeding or preening. If one bird starts to bathe, then its action often causes the others to join in, until most of the flock is bathing. Humans often behave in a similar way. Someone laughing heartily can cause others to laugh with him, even though they may not know what it is that's so funny!

THE LANGUAGE OF BIRDS

Birds "talk" to each other by using a system of signals. They use sound signals and visual signals that others can hear or see. Humans, too, use signs of this sort, in addition to verbal language.

In human signaling, facial expression is very important. Movements of the body, such as gestures and postures, are less significant. A smile or a frown can mean a lot, and a movement of the wrist or a position of the body usually only serves to emphasize a point we are making in some other way. Birds are very different. The expression on a bird's face hardly ever changes, although opening the beak may indicate something. But ruffling the feathers, spreading the wings, or adopting certain body postures mean special things to birds, and are significant. These actions can indicate anger or fear, and whether the bird is going to attack or fly away. These signals make a precise "language" clearly understood by other birds.

Below: Many birds have striking markings that enable other birds of the same species to recognize them. In the Willet (1), European Oystercatcher (2) and American Avocet (3), these markings show during flight, but are hidden when the birds are on the ground or in the water.

BIRD MARKINGS

Every species of bird has its own particular markings which identify it. Birds in flocks will fly toward another bird with the same markings. But birds that travel alone will fly away as soon as they perceive a similar bird.

Markings may attract enemies as well as fellow birds. Thus, many social birds have markings on the tail, rump or wings that are hidden until they spread their wings. On the ground, they are inconspicuous and therefore less vulnerable prey. But the markings are visible as soon as the birds take flight, and help to keep the flock together.

Birds belonging to different species that fly and feed together sometimes have similar markings to help keep them in a group. This is of survival value to all the species involved.

Above: The songs of the Nightingale, Nightjar and Savi's Warbler (top to bottom) are loud and continue without stopping. Although one might think such a noise would attract enemies, these birds are well camouflaged by their plumage and may safely sing at night under cover of darkness.

Above: The European Blackbird (left) has a clear, musical song but sings close to cover so that it cannot be seen. The Ring Ouzel, which lives in open moorland and is more easily spotted, has a crude song that does not easily give away its position.

Left: A male Chaffinch sings to defend its territory. The song informs other birds that the singer is a Chaffinch, is male, is holding some territory it has gained, and that it is singing from its territory and defying others to try and take its territory away. Young Chaffinches have a basic inborn ability to sing, but they learn to sing correctly from other Chaffinches. If a young bird is kept from hearing others of its kind, it will develop a song which lasts the right length of time and has the proper notes but is not phrased correctly. The young bird will only pick up the "correct" Chaffinch phrasing, and will not learn incorrectly by imitating other birds.

CALLING AND SINGING

Making sounds is a very important part of bird signaling systems. Each species has a repertoire of sound signals for different purposes. Titmice have as many as 40 different cries, but most birds make do with one to two dozen. There are two general kinds of cries: *call notes* and *song*.

Call notes can mean many things. One call may mean "Here I am, where are you?" and may be used by birds in a flock to keep together. Special flight calls get birds into the air and both kinds of call notes are especially useful to birds that migrate by night, when it is hard to see. Calls can also mean danger, and warning signals are often similar among different birds. The specific call depends upon the enemy that is approaching. A perched bird of prey, a fox, or a cat, will induce a *mobbing* call that is easy to recognize and tells all the birds around where the enemy is. Mobbing calls sound like "chinks" or "chacks," and the responding birds will gather, or mob, to attack their enemy. Birds of prey on the wing, however, get a danger call that sounds like a high-pitched "see-e-e". This call is not easy to pinpoint, as the caller does not want to expose its own position, but it serves to warn the other birds to flee for cover.

Above: A pair of Australian Gannets preen each other. This action is a way of saying "keep calm," and prevents aggression.

Above: Some oystercatchers "pipe" together for the same reason.

Left: The aggressive display (1) and the appeasement display (2) of the Common Jay are very different. In the appeasement display, the bird points its bill upward to indicate that it is ready to withdraw. The Sandwich Tern points its bill at a rival bird to threaten it (3). To appease a rival, the bird's weapon is pointed away (4).

Below: A male Crimson Finch and a female Zebra Finch communicate by postures. The female has come too close to the male (top), who stretches out his body in a horizontal posture of aggression. The Zebra Finch stands upright (center), on the defensive, and finally flies away (bottom).

Song is a form of language that birds use during the breeding season. A song may attract a female to a male and sharpen her instinct for mating. But the song of the male is just as importantly a warning to other males to keep away. Birds that are otherwise much alike may have very different mating songs so that a female is not attracted to the wrong species of male. The song itself ties in with the bird's way of life. Birds that live in open country do not flout their presence to enemies with songs that easily give away their position. On the other hand, birds that live in woods or thickets and cannot be seen easily, may sing loudly and continuously, apparently heedless of being spotted.

PEACE TALKS

Although living together in groups often presents problems, most social birds have developed behavior patterns which help them avoid fighting. They will generally settle a dispute by exchanging signals to indicate that one bird will abandon a claim and withdraw. The aggressive bird adopts a *display* – a posture or a gesture – expressing his hostility. The peace-making bird adopts an appeasement display, and so combat is avoided.

SETTING ABOUT BREEDING

Breeding is essential for all species of animal. If the animals of one particular species do not produce enough young to make up for their kind that die, then these animals will gradually decrease in number and eventually become extinct. In the 1800's, Passenger Pigeons in North America could have been counted in the millions. Then men killed so many for eating and for decorative purposes that the pigeons could not breed fast enough. They had vanished from the wild by 1900, and the last one in captivity died in a zoo in 1914.

Birds usually breed at a specific time of the year, during what is called the *breeding season*. As the birds gather, each male selects a territory in which to breed. The male must attract a female and the pair must build a nest, hatch the eggs, feed their young, and protect them from enemies. For most birds, this is a time when they must cooperate with each other. Birds that would ordinarily squabble over food or ignore each other must now change their behavior completely.

The changes in behavior are produced by the release of certain chemicals called *hormones* in the bird's body. The release of these hormones is keyed to the changing seasons.

During the breeding season, there is a whole language of "courtship." The birds exchange signals

Above: Yellow-eyed Penguins of New Zealand form couples or pairs that stay together for many years. Observers kept watch on one pair that bred each year for thirteen years. The male is on the left, the female on the right.

Left: The male Ring-necked Pheasant is a brightly colored bird. It takes no part in rearing its young, as its plumage would attract enemies to the nest. The females in the background are dull-colored and less easily seen, and they rear the young.

Below: The Great Bustard attracts a mate by advertising itself — it assumes an odd posture with its feathers splayed out. Normally the male is a drab brownish bird, but when it seeks a female, it suddenly uncovers its magnificent white plumage. The Great Bustard lives in Europe and Asia. It may stand three feet tall and is one of the largest flying birds. Great Bustards are rare birds and are protected by laws.

to mark out territories and attract mates, and also to reduce the mutual feeling of fear that a pair of birds would normally have. Only then can the birds mate, lay their eggs and rear their young.

Most birds split up into pairs to breed. Some pairs breed together year after year; but some birds breed in groups, rather than pairs, and others may have more than one mate. In some species, such as the Old World Painted Snipe, the female may mate with several males. In this species, the males take over the hatching and rearing of the young.

DEFENDING A TERRITORY

Most birds breed in territories which they often have to fight to obtain. Each pair of birds has its own breeding territory and no other birds of the same species are allowed to enter. Small perching birds may command a territory of less than two acres. But the Golden Eagle is master of a vast territory as large as 250 square miles. The males will fight to keep their territory intact. In spring, intruding male European Robins, for example, show off their red breasts as a threat to resident robins. If a red breast is sighted in another bird's territory, it is savagely assaulted. This can happen even if the visitor is not another robin but only a Chaffinch with a pinkish breast.

Right: The Black Grouse attracts its mate by adopting a strange posture and crowing and singing in a bubbling but musical way. The Black Grouse lives in forests in Europe and Asia. The males have special display grounds, called *leks*, where many gather and perform their odd antics to attract the females. Each male has its own territory.

Maintaining territories is important, not only because these are refuges for courting and mating, but also because they may contain the birds' particular food supply. Many birds' territories are larger than they need to feed themselves. But the defended areas become smaller when the bird population in a certain region increases, and this does not seem to affect the breeding.

Birds do not always feed in their own territories. Oystercatchers, for example, have two territories: one is inland, where the birds rear their young; and the other is on the shore, where the adults feed. The parents commute between the two territories to bring food to their young. Many sea birds use their small nesting areas for mating and for rearing chicks. But these birds fly far and wide in search of food and do not have specific feeding territories. Many finches and birds that eat insects on the wing behave in this way also.

Although fighting over territories makes pairs of birds space themselves out to breed, the territories often adjoin so that they form "neighborhoods" of breeding birds. Not all birds have large individual territories. Black-headed Gulls nest in colonies where the nests are about three feet apart. Nesting too closely gives enemies such as Carrion Crows a better chance of finding the eggs. But if the nests are too far apart, the gulls would not come to each other's aid in case of attack.

Left: Great Crested Grebes have several kinds of display for courtship. The "penguin" dance is a lively intricate dance in which both birds rush together, rear up face to face, and dive to bring up pieces of vegetation in their beaks.

Opposite page: Crowned Cranes have a wild courtship dance in which they leap and prance. These cranes live in Africa and migrate north for the summer. When the cranes arrive at their summer home, they split up into pairs and the dances commence. The male moves toward the female, bowing, with his neck bent forward. Then he leaps into the air several times, making trumpeting calls. His mate joins in, splashing about in the shallow water where the dances take place.

Above and opposite page: North Atlantic Gannets have several courtship displays. Bowing (1 and 2) is done by the male bird to draw a female's attention to a nest site. It consists of head-shaking, followed by bowing, and keeps away other males. Male advertising (3) brings the females to the nest site. It is a less aggressive posture. Facing away (4) is the female's gesture when she intrudes into the male's territory. The female hides her bill, a peaceful gesture, to win the male's confidence. Mutual fencing (5 and 6) involves dipping, mainly by the male, and crossing the bills like scissors. This reduces fear and aggression. Sky pointing (7 and 8) is a signal given when one bird is about to leave. It is a sign to the other bird to stay, so that the nest is not left unguarded.

Left: Many displays that birds perform come from the first part of the take-off leap. A Mallard Duck adopts a posture with its head and tail up (1). This is one of many postures that make up the courtship ritual of the Mallard. A Mute Swan threatens a rival (2). A Cormorant flaps its wings rhythmically to show off the white patches on its thighs (3). The courtship posture of the Hooded Merganser involves putting its head back (4). All these postures are derived from the first part of the take-off leap.

Above: A diagram of a bird about to take off. It coils itself up like a spring before leaping into the air.

ATTRACTING A MATE

Once a bird is on its territory and has a nesting site, it must lure a mate there to breed. There is strong competition for good spots, so a bird cannot ever relax vigilance to keep a site. The male must announce its presence to other males to keep them away, as well as to female birds to attract them.

Birds can use song to do this, and those that live among trees and bushes or under cover of darkness will sing loudly and continuously to proclaim their territories and call for mates. The song also serves to

Right: Birds perform several courtship displays that are similar to the second part of the take-off leap. The Goldeneye has a display in which it stretches out its body on top of the water (1). The Great Crested Grebe has a threatening display that consists of stretching its body forward (2). This display is given to a rival bird. The displays of the Gray Heron also have a stretch phase (3). The Hooded Merganser also assumes a stretching posture as part of its courtship (4). This bird therefore has postures that come from both the first and second parts of the take-off leap. The posture that comes from the first part is shown on the opposite page.

Above: A diagram of a bird making the second part of its take-off leap. After coiling up like a spring, the bird straightens out, arrow-like, as it leaps into the air. Its final position resembles the final position of a clean dive into a swimming pool.

tell the female where the male is located. The "foghorn" call of the Bittern, for example, booms out over the reed beds like a beacon of sound. Every day during the breeding season, birds re-establish their territories at dawn and sunset with a boisterous chorus of song.

But song is not the only language that a bird can use to court its mate. It may have special plumage and adopt unusual postures to lure a female. Many birds use both sound and visual language in courtship, but some rely entirely on their physical appearance. Their striking markings are shown off to best advantage to attract a mate.

Below: Like the Shelduck (left) the male Mandarin Duck has a courtship ritual that is similar to preening. But the Mandarin Duck simply touches its sail-like wing feather with its bill, instead of burying its bill in its rump feathers.

Above: The courtship gestures of some ducks are similar to the movements they make when preening. The bird bends its head as if to take some oil from its oil gland. In courting, this is a nervous gesture, performed when the male is uncertain about the response of the female.

COURTSHIP CEREMONIES

Any gentleman knows that he must behave in a certain way to appeal to a lady, although exactly what he must do depends to some extend on the particular society in which he lives. Birds also have all sorts of ceremonies to accompany "courtship". A pair of birds establishes and maintains a bond by exchanging signals which reduce the fear and aggression that would normally be present.

Some of the most beautiful courtship ceremonies are performed by the Great Crested Grebe. In the "cat" display a courting bird adopts a cat-like defensive posture. In the "penguin" dance, the two

Right: Two Herring Gulls face away from each other. This is a movement that reduces aggression between the birds. Herring Gulls are aggressive birds and their aggression must be quelled if the birds are ever to get together to breed. Facing away happens early in the courtship, when the two birds are not completely used to each other. Turning the head away like this hides the bill from the partner, and is an important peacemaking ceremony.

Opposite page: A Herring Gull tears up some tussocks of grass. This bird has been confronted by another male in a dispute about territory. Its impulse to attack is not yet strong enough to actually do so, and instead, it rips up the grass. This is ritual behavior and serves to warn the opponent. If the latter does not retreat, more direct action is taken.

birds rush toward each other, rear up breast to breast, and dive to pick up pieces of weed in their beaks! (See page 38.) Two mated birds may also perform a head-shaking ceremony. Such ceremonies have grown out of other behavior patterns and have evolved into rituals with special and strong meanings. The rituals are "exaggerated" so that their meanings cannot be misinterpreted.

To go with these exaggerated movements and postures, birds may have special markings that increase the impact on their mates. A peacock display during the breeding season, for instance, is a magnificent sight to behold.

Rituals may be derived from several kinds of behavior. Stylized versions of movements normally used while drinking or preening can become parts of courtship ceremonies. The way a bird takes off on a flight gives rise to many kinds of displays (see pages 40 and 41). For some birds, a whole series of take-off leaps have evolved into courtship dances. The male Gouldian Finches of Australia perform a jerking dance in front of the females. By ruffling up their plumage to frame their heads in cobalt blue, and enlarging their lilac breast patches, the finches look quite spectacular. The male Zebra Finch does a dance in which it hops toward the female and then turns away, twisting its body back and forth all the time. This ritual of approaching and avoiding another bird is widely used during courtship.

Above: Birds perform many gestures during their courtship that may seem to have nothing to do with the courtship itself. The Spice Finch (top) has a special posture called the low twist, which is a beak wipe that never actually gets performed. The bird stops before the beak rubs against the perch. The Madagascar Lovebird (center) often scratches its head. This is normal behavior in lovebirds which, contrary to their name, are often hostile to their mates. But the Black-masked Lovebird (bottom) scratches as a courtship gesture. It raises its foot to its red bill, possibly to draw attention to its brightly colored plumage.

Left: A male Red Avadavat goes through a courtship ritual that is similar to its nest-building movements. It takes a piece of twig in its beak as it bows to the female. This display comes from the movements that the avadavat makes as it tucks in twigs to build its nest. These pretty little birds live in Asia and their strange name is a corruption of Ahmadabad, the Indian city from where the first avadavats were sent to Europe. They live in flocks in marsh land and wet grassland. Red Avadavats make readily tamed cage birds.

Certain activities during courtship seem unrelated to the purpose of breeding. A bird may suddenly scratch, wipe its beak, or preen its feathers. (See the ducks shown on page 42.) These movements, called displacement activities, actually help to relieve anxiety. People have similar release valves. Scratching the head, tapping the feet, and whistling, often help in a difficult situation. In some species, the courtship ritual looks as if it has evolved out of such displacement activities.

If a bird's courtship is successful, it is soon followed by the building of a nest. It is not surprising, then, to learn that some courtship ceremonies include behavior that has to do with nest-building. The "penguin" dance of the Great Crested Grebes, in which the birds pick up pieces of weed, is an example. Herons, too, pass nest material to each other during courtship.

Left: An Adélie Penguin offers its mate a pebble. Stones are valuable objects to possess in the snowy wastes of Antarctica where these penguins live, as nothing else is available to build nests. Gathering pebbles is the part of the nest-building routine which has also become part of the birds' courtship behavior. The pebbles are often stolen from the nest pile of a neighboring penguin! Adélie Penguins return to the same colony to breed every year, and they build their nest of pebbles on almost the same spot every time.

TURNING INSTINCTS INTO RITUALS

When their instincts are aroused, birds react in
ways that can be compared with human blushing
or perspiring. In birds, the ruffling of feathers is a
way of cooling the body when it gets overheated.
This kind of bodily reaction can also become part
of the courtship behavior pattern.

Turkeys blush to attract a mate. They also
(as do several birds) raise the feathers all over their
bodies as they strut about. Other birds ruffle only
certain parts of their plumage – parts which usually
have markings that stand out when feathers are
ruffled. Sometimes raising the feathers may reveal
these special hidden markings that attract the
attention of a prospective mate.

Certain species have displays of feathers that are
particularly striking. These birds show off beautiful
crests, beards, tufts, plumes, and trains of feathers.
The region of the body carrying the especially attractive markings or outgrowths is the one that is turned
toward the potential mate.

The Golden Pheasant turns itself sideways because
it has a superb cape of golden plumage around its
neck that is best seen from the side. The Peacock
spreads a magnificent fan of iridescent feathers to
frame its bright blue head and neck. This is an

irresistible sight to the Peahen when it sees the Peacock from the front. The Argus Pheasant, instead of erecting its tail into a fan, uses its long and beautifully marked wing feathers to form a wide circle around its head.

ACTING LIKE A BABY

Some courtship rituals are very strange and involve one bird behaving as if it were a baby bird. Usually it is the female that begs food from the male in the same way that the young birds in the nest get food from their parents, though male Red Avadavats use the same wing movement when courting females as they did when they wanted to be fed while still very young. Perhaps the "acting young" of one bird makes the other feel like a parent, and thus dispels any fear or aggression.

HOLDING COURT

Most birds form pairs that stay together for the breeding season. But some birds only come together to mate for a few short moments during the season and otherwise live apart.

Above: Many male birds have special feathers that they use to attract the attention of the female. The male Capercaillie (top) has a beard. Leadbeater's Cockatoo of Australia (center) raises a superb crest of red and pink feathers as part of its courtship. The Blue crowned Pigeon of New Guinea wears a permanent crown of blue lacy feathers. It is a huge pigeon, nearly three feet in length.

Opposite page: A male European Goldfinch stands over a female and offers her food as she sits on the nest. This is courtship behavior and takes place before mating. It comes from the behavior characteristic of the parent-young relationship. Courtship feeding is a ritual followed by many birds. Usually the female sits on a nest and begs her food from the male, just as she begged food from her parents when she was young. This kind of behavior helps to keep the birds together. If the female sits on the eggs all the time, "free" feeding like this is essential. Hornbills build their nests around the female, who has to be fed in this way.

This brief union is achieved in a strange way. The males gather at special display grounds called *arenas* or *leks*. Each bird in the lek defends a small plot of its own called a *court*. The size of the lek varies. The Greater Prairie Chickens of North America carry out their displays in an arena as large as two hundred yards by eight hundred yards long. An arena this size holds about four hundred male birds. Most male "lek" birds have splendid plumage that they show off in their courts to attract the females. But they also spend much time displaying to each other to maintain their positions in their temporary all-male society. When the females arrive, they take their choice of the males on display. They may fly from lek to lek before finally retiring to lay their eggs.

Ruffs are unusual lek birds of Europe and Asia that get their name from the large collars or ruffs of colored feathers around their heads and necks. The ruffs vary in color from black to brown to red to yellow to white. None of the males is exactly like another, and telling them apart is easy. The males also behave in different ways. Some males are *resident* males, aggressive birds with dark-colored ruffs, that hold their own courts. There are also *satellite* males

that do not have their own courts, but associate with resident males. The satellite males are less aggressive than the resident males and usually have white-colored ruffs that attract females to the court – but usually to the resident male, not the satellite male. At a large lek, only the resident males mate. But at smaller leks, the presence of satellite males increases the chances of mating for both resident males and satellite males.

Some lek birds have magnificent plumage to attract the females. One of these is the bright red male Cock-of-the-Rock. The female has the same size plumage, but is brown. The Superb Lyre Bird, a spectacular arena bird, is one of two kinds of lyre birds that live in Australia. Each male clears up to ten courts in the undergrowth. The females are enticed into them. As the male proceeds with the display, it brings its ornate silvery tail over its head like a "fairy parasol." A lyre bird adopting this pose is a sight of rare and moving beauty.

Birds of Paradise, which come from New Guinea and northern Australia, are some of the most beautiful birds in the world. There are some 40 distinct species and at least 24 of these display in arenas. The Birds of Paradise attract their mates by a fantastic show of feathers. The adornments are amazingly varied – strange long plumes that fall like ribbons from the tail or head and sprays of lacy feathers that form beautiful mists of color. The bird's display posturing and behavior show its beauty to the fullest. The Magnificent Bird of Paradise is so "vain" that it pulls leaves away from the undergrowth around its court so that more light will reflect onto its glistening plumage.

But Birds of Paradise are not the only birds that go to such lengths to charm their mates. Other notable wooers (related to Birds of Paradise) live in the same part of the globe. These are the amazing Bowerbirds.

Below: The male Satin Bowerbird builds an avenue along which the female, shown behind, must be enticed before mating takes place. The avenues are extremely intricate. The male bird first clears a space in the undergrowth, and covers the space with a mat of sticks and twigs. Then it builds two parallel fences of upright sticks which are stuck firmly in the ground and entwined together, sometimes bending over to meet overhead. The fences are spaced far enough apart for the female to walk into the avenue. The floor is decorated with blue objects such as flowers and feathers. The inside of the walls of the avenue is daubed with a blue or green "paint", made by mixing charcoal and other pigments with saliva. The bowerbird, one of a few species which can use a tool, applies the paint by holding a wad of bark in its beak. After mating, the female leaves the avenue to build a nest, and hatches and rears the young on her own. Outside the breeding season, these bowerbirds travel throughout eastern Australia in small flocks of four to six birds. They live on berries and fruits, as well as insects.

BLOSSOMS, BIRDS AND BOWERS

Bowerbirds are not as spectacular as the Birds of Paradise. In a few of the 19 existing species, the males have special head plumes and bright colors, but most are fairly dull in appearance. They make up for this by building special bowers of twigs and sticks which are then decorated with flowers and plants, and even painted. The skill of the Bowerbird as an architect and decorator is unmatched anywhere in the animal world.

But, skilled though it is as a builder, the male Bowerbird does not build the nest. Its carefully constructed bower is intended only for mating purposes. The female Bowerbird is lured into the bower to mate, and after its visit, it goes off alone to build a nest, lay its eggs and bring up the young.

Two species of Bowerbirds do not construct bowers at all. Three species called "stage-makers"

Above: Stage-maker Bowerbirds are the simplest of the bowerbirds. They clear courts in the undergrowth and decorate them with fresh leaves from certain kinds of trees. The Tooth-billed, or Stage-maker, Bowerbird cuts the leaves off trees with the saw-like notches along its bill and places them with the pale sides uppermost on the ground. If the leaves are turned over, the male bowerbird will replace them with the pale side up. As the leaves wither, the bird gets fresh ones and the court becomes surrounded by a circle of discarded dead leaves. The bird spends much time singing and calling from a perch above his court, trying to attract a female. It is a good mimic.

Left: The Birds of Paradise from the New Guinea region are among the most ornamental birds in the world. These three Birds of Paradise are the Magnificent Riflebird (1), the King of Saxony's Bird of Paradise (2), and the Magnificent Bird of Paradise (3). They are birds that display in arenas, and are shown here in display postures. The Magnificent Bird of Paradise makes its display even more astonishing by trimming away the leaves around its court so that more light can reach its glistening plumage.

Right: The Crestless Gardener is a bowerbird of western New Guinea. The male displays on a court to attract the female to mate, and entices her there by building a magnificent bower three to six feet high. This bowerbird is one of several such birds called Maypole builders. It begins by piling up a pyramid of twigs and sticks around the foot of a small tree. It then builds a tent-like hut over the pyramid and constructs a low stockade to mark out a "garden" in front of its hut. The bowerbird then decorates the floor of its bower, the pyramid inside and the garden with flowers and other plants, berries and snail shells. The bird even replaces wilted flowers with fresh ones! The female is enticed into this enchanting "love nest" to mate, after which she leaves to lay her eggs and bring up the young. These bowerbirds may return to their bowers year after year and repair and extend them. Large bowers may take several years to complete.

build the simplest bowers by clearing a "stage" in the undergrowth three to six feet across, rather like a miniature circus ring. The bird adorns the area with leaves, and one stage-maker even erects a curtain of bamboo and ferns around it.

Five Bowerbird species are called Maypole builders, because their bowers are built around tree trunks in the fashion of Maypole dancers constructing a fan of ribbons around a pole. Some of the Maypole builders are called gardeners because they plant mosses in and around their bowers, and decorate their courts with ferns and blossoms, replacing them with fresh plants as the old ones wilt. The bowers may be repaired and extended every year, and can reach a height of almost ten feet.

The remaining 9 species are called avenue builders. They construct walled avenues of twigs and sticks; two of these species actually daub the walls with a paint composed of saliva and pigments! They pick up wads of leaves or bark to use as brushes, and are among the very few kinds of birds that use tools.

NESTING AND LOOKING AFTER THE YOUNG

After courtship and mating, birds must build nests to contain the eggs, and later house the hatched infant birds until they are old enough to take care of themselves. In many species, males and females gather materials together and weave them into a nest. But many birds are less cooperative with one another. The males are required to do most of the work in species such as weaverbirds and grassfinches. In the manakins, vireos, hummingbirds and finches, the female is the homebuilder.

Nest-building is hard work. Barn Swallows make nests shaped like flasks and plastered with mud, often in the rafters of barns or sheds. Bird watchers have observed that a pair of swallows make more than 1,200 trips to carry enough mud to the nest site. The nest of the Black-throated Oriole may contain more than three thousand separate pieces of material! All this requires energy, and the work must proceed on schedule for the nest to be finished when the eggs are laid. The activity and scheduling of nest-building is triggered by certain events.

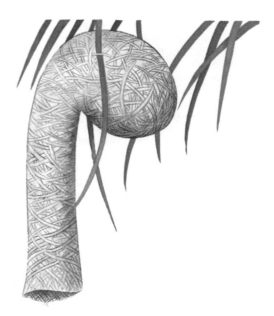

Above: Some weaverbirds build intricate nests with entrance tunnels hanging down below a nesting chamber.

Below left: The female canary starts to build a nest as the days get longer and courtship begins (1). Her brood patch then becomes sensitive (2) and for relief she lines the nest with soft feathers (3).

Above: Social Weavers of South Africa work together, as many as six hundred at a time, to build huge communal nests in trees.

Nest-building in canaries provides a good example. Their nests are built in two parts. The females build a cup of rough grass and twigs and then line it with soft feathers to make it comfortable. The bird starts to feel the need to build a nest when a chemical called *estrogen*, which is a female hormone, builds up in her body. This happens as the daylight hours increase day by day – that is, in the spring. In addition, the courtship of the male canary intensifies at this time and helps to produce more estrogen. The female starts building the nest. As she does so, the accumulation of estrogen has the side effect of causing her to lose some feathers from her breast, leaving bare brood patches which become quite sensitive as egg-laying time approaches. By now, the canary has completed the rough cup. But the grass and twigs scratch the sensitive brood patches as she tries to sit on the nest, so she finishes off the nest by lining it with feathers. The soft feathers keep her and the nestlings comfortable, and the mother bird's warm brood patches efficiently heat the eggs as she sits on them.

NESTS, NESTS, NESTS

There are almost as many different kinds of nests as there are different species of birds. Some birds do not build any nests at all. King Penguins and Emperor Penguins lay single eggs which the males hold

Right: The Indian Tailorbird stitches its home together like a tailor using a needle and thread. The bird pierces holes at the edges of some large green leaves, knots fibers of cotton or other plant fibers, and threads the ends through the holes with its beak. Then it pulls the threads to draw the leaves together to form a cup, which it lines with soft materials to make a nest.

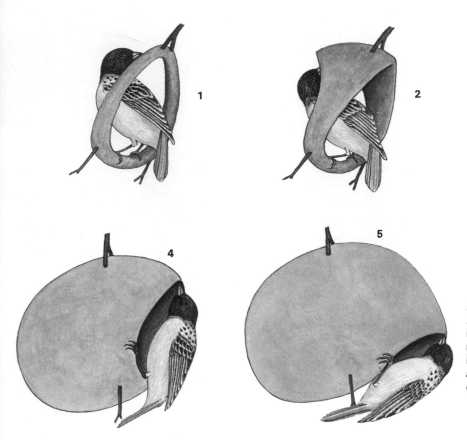

Above left: The male Village Weaver of Africa builds its nest of palm fibers torn in thin strips from palm fronds. He first makes a ring (1) and enlarges it (2) into an egg chamber (3). A small antechamber (4) and an entrance (5) complete the nest.

between their feet and under-folds of skin on their bellies. At the other extreme are the Social Weavers. A community of as many as three hundred pairs of birds may work together and build a vast umbrella-shaped nest to house an entire colony. Other notable nest-builders are the megapodes of Australia, New Guinea and the Philippines. These birds bury their eggs in immense mounds of rotting plants, which provide the heat to keep the eggs warm. The largest mounds may be as much as 16 yards across!

The form of a nest may often depend on how safe the nest site is from enemies. Guillemots inhabiting ledges on cliffs feel secure there, so they do not build any nests at all. Some perching birds of the tropics construct nests with long entrance tunnels that look like socks hanging upside-down from a clothesline, a contrivance which prevents snakes and other enemies from entering the nests.

Birds use all sorts of materials to make nests. Twigs and grass are easy to find in the countryside. Some swiftlets manufacture their nests almost entirely of their own saliva. Some swallows use mud; the Eider Duck uses fibers, stones and feathers; some penguins make nests only of pebbles; and Crested Flycatchers even use snake-skins!

INCUBATING THE EGGS

Each of the eggs produced by a mated female bird contains a live embryo bird. (The eggs available at markets come from unmated female chickens, and do not contain embryos.) The embryo must be kept warm inside the egg. It lives on the yolk and grows until it fills the interior of the shell, at which time it is ready to hatch. If the egg is not looked after and warmed, the embryo will die before it has a chance to hatch. The time that an embryo chick spends inside the egg developing into a hatchling is called the *incubation period*. This period is only about ten days for small perching birds. The Royal Albatross has the longest known incubation period – 80 days.

Most birds have brood patches which fit over the eggs and keep them warm. Gannets and cormorants have especially warm feet with which to incubate the eggs. Female birds usually have the task of incubating. Male Hornbills make sure it gets done by sealing the female into the nest together with the eggs! A small hole is left open in the nest so that the male can feed the female. Male birds that are brightly colored must not spend much time near the nest for fear of attracting enemies. The incubating is best left to their more camouflaged mates. In more than half the families of birds, however, both males and females share the task of incubating.

Not all birds use their own body heat to incubate eggs. The megapodes of Australasia bury their eggs in mounds of rotting plants like giant compost heaps. The eggs must be kept at 92°F., whatever the weather outside the mound. For the temperature to remain constant, the male bird must work as long as 13

Above: The Mallee Fowl of Australia buries its eggs under a mound of rotting plants. This material keeps the eggs warm, and so the Mallee Fowl does not have to sit on its eggs to hatch them. The bird instinctively knows that it must add more plants at night, when it is cold, to keep the eggs warm (right), and scrape some away in the morning (left), when the air gets warmer.

Below: A female Whitethroat shows no concern for an egg that has dropped out of the nest. Several other birds also seemingly accept such occurrences with indifference. These birds are not really stupid or heartless, since getting the displaced egg back into the nest could serve little purpose, as the shell is almost certainly broken.

Above: The King Penguin does not build a nest. It keeps its egg warm by holding the egg on its feet and enveloping it in a fold of skin. The Emperor Penguin incubates its egg in the same way. These birds are the largest penguins and have only one egg. Nesting materials are hard to find in the icy southern wastes where they live, and so they have found a way of doing without a nest. The embryo penguin develops inside the egg as long as it is kept warm. But if the egg is exposed for even a moment to the freezing temperatures, the embryo dies. The incubation period lasts for more than 60 days, during which time the male penguin guards the egg without eating. During incubation the female is away feeding. As soon as the young penguin hatches out, the female returns to take charge and the male goes off to eat.

Right: The Common European Cuckoo is one of several species of birds that lay their eggs in the nests of other birds.

hours every day. He scrapes material away from the top of the mound if it should become too warm inside (it may reach 113°F.), allowing heat to escape. In the evening he builds up the mound, preventing the cold night air from getting to the eggs inside.

In this way, the male keeps the eggs from being chilled or baked. To do so, he must first determine the temperature inside the mound. The megapode does this by taking samples of soil or compost from the mound and pressing the sample against its heat-sensitive palate or tongue. Their incubation period is a long one – up to 8 or 9 weeks. When the baby megapodes eventually hatch, they wriggle their way up through the mounds to the air.

Other birds behave in a similar way to the megapodes. The Mallee Fowl of Australia bury their eggs in mounds. Zoologists studied this fowl by placing an electric heating element inside its mound. They found that the fowl scraped away soil from the mound as soon as the heater was switched on. In this way, it was proven that the male bird was responding to temperature changes inside the mound and not to any other factor.

The Maleo Fowl of the Celebes islands in Indonesia lays its eggs one by one in the black volcanic sand of the beaches there. The sand absorbs the heat of the sun which is sufficient to cause the eggs to incubate. This bird may also bury its eggs near active volcanoes where the soil is warmed by steam – just like central heating!

Above: A young cuckoo.

Above: A cuckoo egg (left) and the egg of its foster parent, a Reed Warbler (right), look very much alike.

STRANGERS IN THE NEST

Some birds do not build nests and do not bring up young. They survive by laying their eggs in the nests of other birds and letting these foster parents rear their young for them. These brood parasites, as they are called, include Black-headed Ducks, honey guides, cowbirds, weaverbirds, viduine weavers, and 47 species of cuckoos.

Each species of parasite bird usually selects a particular species of host bird in whose nest it lays its eggs. The eggs of both birds must be about the same size and color, and both must have about the same incubation period. The young intruder must receive the right food, but it makes certain signals so that the foster parent feeds the parasite along with its own young, and sometimes even at their expense.

The European Cuckoo is a well-known brood parasite. It lays its eggs in the nests of more than 120 other species of birds. But each female cuckoo probably only uses one species of host bird. It lays only one egg in the host's nest, and removes one of the eggs already in the nest to fool the foster parent. A cuckoo that lays brown eggs will place its egg in the nest of a meadow pipit, which also lays brown eggs. Cuckoos that have bluish eggs will lay them in the nests of hedge sparrows, where they blend with the sparrow's own blue eggs.

Once the young cuckoo hatches, it asserts itself.

Left: The male Paradise Whydah (left) displays elaborate courtship postures. Paradise Whydahs live in Africa, and lay their eggs in the nests of Melba Finches (above). But they only use the geographic races of these finches that live in the southern and eastern parts of their range. The female lays two or three eggs in the host's nest. Unlike cuckoos, the young whydahs do not push their foster brothers and sisters out of the nest.

Left: The male Pin-tailed Whydah calls the attention of the female to a male Violet-eared Waxbill that is building a nest. Whydahs lay their eggs in the nests of waxbills, and the parent waxbills rear the young whydahs. The relationship between the two species of birds is very close. The female whydah does not feel like breeding until she sees the male waxbill preparing to breed. The call that the male whydah uses to attract her attention to the waxbill is very similar to the nest call of the waxbill itself. Female whydahs, in fact, prefer to mate with male whydahs that can imitate waxbills in this way!

The other young birds are ruthlessly tossed out of the nest and thus they will not compete with the alien bird for food. The young cuckoo has a huge yellow mouth with great fleshy flanges on both sides. The sight of this spurs the foster parents into bringing food. Such is its appetite that one intruding cuckoo can eat as much as the whole brood it displaces.

The European Cuckoo and other cuckoos of the Old World are the best-known of the fully parasite birds. In North and South America, most cuckoos raise their own young and only the Yellow-billed Cuckoo and the Black-billed Cuckoo occasionally lay eggs in other nests. The main parasite birds in the New World are the cowbirds. In Africa, the honey guides are savagely effective as parasites. The young honey guides are born with sharp hooks on their bills, which they use to kill the other birds in the nest. The hooks drop off as soon as this grisly work is done. Honey guide eggs are laid one to a nest. If more than one honey guide were to hatch in a nest, one would kill the other.

This behavior may seem wicked on the part of the parasite and stupid on the part of the host bird. But both are behaving instinctively in a way that over a long period has the greatest survival value.

Below: A Black-headed Gull removes pieces of egg shell from its nest. This action helps the gull and its young to survive. The inside of the egg is white, and any pieces of egg shell lying about will stand out. If the shells were not removed, enemies such as Carrion Crows (below left) would see the white fragments against the dark nest, and would attack the newly hatched birds. Therefore, the parent gull carries the egg shells to a safe distance from the nest shortly after the young hatch out. Not all gulls take this precaution. Herring Gulls are large, ferocious birds and can take care of enemies, so they need not get rid of telltale egg shells. Kittiwakes nest on sheer cliff faces, where they are rarely bothered by Carrion Crows.

BODYGUARDS

Birds are very much concerned with keeping their young out of danger. The position of the nest and the way it is hidden by camouflage help to keep enemies away. But some birds use other means to protect their young.

Several species of birds, such as auks, gulls and herons, nest with their own kind in colonies, finding safety in numbers. Other birds team up with more aggressive birds, which act as "bodyguards."

In South America, small tanagers and tyrant flycatchers will nest near aggressive birds such as the Kiskadee, which has no fear of raiders. Redtailed Hawks, Marabou Storks, Snowy Owls and Pied Crows often have more defenseless birds nesting near them for protection.

Right: In South America, Yellow-rumped Caciques build their nests alongside hanging wasps' nests, thus obtaining protection from enemies. Other animals are not likely to attack a wasps' nest, and both nests look very much alike.

Some birds even live with aggressive insects for protection. Black-throated Warblers and Yellow-rumped Caciques nest among the hanging nests of hornets and wasps. Weaverbirds build strange nests that can easily be seen by enemies, and so they, too, live among wasps' nests. This association helps to protect the birds, but it seems of little advantage to the insects. The birds often burrow into their breeding places to build nests, and sometimes even eat the wasps!

Right: An American Robin feeds its young. The young birds sit with their mouths wide open, ready to gobble up as many worms as the parents can find. The chicks depend entirely on the adult birds for nourishment. To get the food, the young must respond with the correct signals. The parent has the food, but to be fed, the hungry chick must behave in a certain way that the parent bird can recognize. Their behavior is instinctive, and so it usually succeeds. After about two weeks the chicks get their feathers and start to fly. American Robins breed in the northern United States and Canada, and migrate south to the southern United States and Central America. Their return traditionally heralds the arrival of spring. The American Robin has a full red front, unlike the European Robin which is red only on the upper part of its breast. It is twice the size of the European Robin, and is seen more often close to cities than in the open country.

People, too, help to protect young birds. Pigeons, martins, swifts, swallows, weavers, sparrows and starlings use the ledges and crevices of buildings as sites for nesting. The White Stork of Europe has been regarded since the Middle Ages as a bird that brings good luck. Because of this superstition, people have always protected the White Stork in Holland and other countries to the east. With the encouragement and protection they receive, White Storks are common in these countries and build nests on the rooftops there. But few White Storks are now to be seen in France, where there is no tradition of protection for storks.

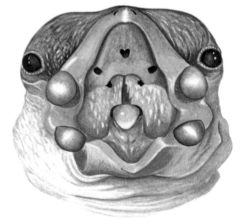

Right: A baby Parrot Finch opens its mouth wide. Baby birds know only one thing: when they are hungry, they gape. The response of the parent is just as instinctive, and it stuffs the open mouth with food until it closes again. This Parrot Finch has a special gape display. The four bright blue spots show up when the chick opens its mouth, and this signal produces an irresistible impulse in the parent to feed the chick. The spots also serve as a guide for the parent's bill during the feeding, and they stop the bird from feeding chicks of the wrong species. The spots disappear when the finch is about five or six weeks old. Gape markings such as this occur in many species of birds. Even if there are no special markings, the inside of the chick's mouth is often brightly colored, a signal to the parent to find food and push it down the young bird's throat.

SIGNALING FOR FOOD

Some birds, such as ducks and game birds, hatch from their shells in an advanced stage of development. They need less attention than other infant birds and can soon feed themselves and fly. But the chicks of most birds depend entirely on their parents to bring them nourishing food. They must beg and signal appropriately to the parents in order to obtain food. This is not difficult; it comes instinctively to the young birds.

Newborn Herring Gull chicks peck at a red spot on the lower mandible of the parent bird's bill, a signal to the parent to give the food in its bill to the chick. Many birds have young that cannot see where the parent's bill is, but as soon as they feel any movement in the nest, the young birds open their mouths and crane their necks in various directions. Only when their eyes eventually open can they direct their mouths toward the parent.

The young bird's open mouth is a strong signal to the parent bird, which responds by stuffing the opening with food. Many infant birds have brightly colored "gapes", or special markings around their mouths, that help to strengthen this signal which shows the parent bird where to put the food. The tongue of a baby Horned Lark, for example, is adorned with jet-black spots and bars. These markings disappear when the birds are a few weeks old.

Some birds know by instinct which are their young. Zoologists find it difficult to trick waxbills by exchanging their young for chicks of another species. But lovebirds learn about their young from what their first brood is like. If their first chicks are taken away and chicks of another species substituted, then the lovebirds will reject any chicks they later have in favor of substitute species given them initially.

Some birds nest in holes where the young are difficult to see. The parent birds respond mainly to the sounds the young make. If a recording of the hunger calls of several chicks is played to a pair of Pied Flycatchers, they will fetch huge quantities of insects, far more than their single chick actually needs.

FAMILY LIFE

Feeding is only one of the many things that a parent bird must do to rear its young. It has to provide extensive care, starting the moment the small, wet and cold baby bird breaks out of its egg. The parent must first warm it with its body until it dries out. Then the parent must defend it from many natural enemies until it is ready to leave the nest. And until the fledgling is ready to live on its own, it must be continually protected for it to grow into an adult.

Above: Scientists tried to find out if Arctic Tern chicks peck at colors that remind them of their food. They constructed imitation bird heads and beaks in various colors, and placed strips of colored paper in the beaks to look like fish. They found that the chicks' favorite combination was a silver bill with a red "fish". This shows that as long as the color combination is appropriate, the colors need not be oriented, as in the natural feeding situation.

To look after its family of young properly, a bird must feel the need to protect them. This urge is brought out by certain characteristics the young possess. By either behavior or appearance the young "encourage" their parents to act like parents.

Many birds are normally very aggressive toward one another and fight over mates and territories. Therefore, a young bird must "show" its parent that it is not after its territory or mate, or else the adult bird may attack it. The young birds are fed and protected because they usually look different from their parents. Young Zebra Finches have black bills that become red when they grow up. If a baby bird's black beak is painted red to look like an adult beak, its parents will mistake it for an adult and the young bird will find itself hungry and ignored.

As the young of aggressive birds grow up and begin to look more like adult birds, they may tend to "annoy" the parents. The young birds then continue their infantile behavior, showing that they are not adults and preventing their parents from

becoming aggressive toward them. Young Herring Gulls develop a special posture to indicate their submission to the parents, which is the same as one the adults use in courtship. It becomes less effective as the birds get older and more self-sufficient.

Some birds are actually "bullied" into behaving properly toward their offspring. Whenever a Night Heron returns to its nest, it bows to its mate and to its young. The young birds recognize their parent by this gesture. If the Night Heron for any reason exhibits an aggressive sort of gesture instead, then the young birds will attack their own parent!

Nestlings that are helpless when they are hatched face many grave dangers. To protect them, birds often nest in places that are difficult to reach, such as cliff ledges. Large numbers of the birds assemble to breed on these sites. Although flocks of birds, as

Above: Parent birds must recognize their young as miniature birds if they are to behave in a parental way towards them and so protect them. Adult Zebra Finches have scarlet bills, whereas their offspring, for the first few weeks of life, have black bills. If the black bill of a young bird is painted red, the male adult will mistake it for an adult female and will try to court the young bird. In addition, the black-billed young will be fed by the parents first and the red-billed fledgling will have to wait for food, no matter how noisily it begs (above right). The paint can soon be removed and the young bird is none the worse for its strange experience. The experiment shows that very simple things, in this case bill color, easily influence the way in which parent birds react to their young. Special markings in young birds also serve to inform the adults that the chicks are not competing with them for anything, and so reduce any hostile feelings that the parents might have.

such, tend to attract enemies, the nests on the cliffs are so hard to reach that the young birds are safe.

Birds that nest together in colonies will come to each other's aid if any enemy approaches. Gulls, terns and skuas will join forces to mob and harry a fox. They will screech at the top of their voices and swoop down on the intruder, flying to within a few inches of its face before wheeling away. Some birds will even attack and draw blood from humans who venture too close to their nests.

The Golden Plover manages to fool its enemies even more cunningly. It draws attention away from its nest by running with its wing dragging on the ground, as if it were broken. Seeing the plover as an easy prey, the hunter follows it. But when it is a safe distance from the nest, the plover quickly flies away.

Another strange way of protecting a family of young birds is practiced by wading birds such as the Purple Sandpiper. This bird lives in extreme northern regions. Its prime enemy is the Arctic fox. The principal food of this fox, however, is rodents. If an Arctic fox comes close to the nest of a Purple Sandpiper, the parent runs off hunched up and with mincing steps, looking very much like a rodent. The predator is thus tempted away from the nest.

NURSERIES

Birds are still in danger after they have left the nest, but are not yet fully grown. Some young birds gather in groups that can be compared to nurseries or kindergartens, and thus are better able to protect themselves. Young Eider Ducks, flamingos and penguins look after themselves this way.

Above: Young birds often have to be protected from their parents as well as from their natural enemies. Adult European Robins are very aggressive birds, and are provoked into instant attack by the sight of the red breast of a rival robin. If the young bird also had a red breast, it would not stand a chance of survival. For their own protection, young robins are dull brown in color.

Right: The young Night Heron (right) has plumage that hides it from view, unlike its parent (left), which can be seen easily. This helps the young bird in situations where danger threatens. An adult heron flees quickly when it is about to be attacked. The young heron is not strong or fast enough to escape in this way, and so it crouches down instead. With luck, the young bird's camouflaged plumage will hide it from the eyes of its enemies.

LEARNING ABOUT LIFE

The way a bird behaves is often a matter of life or death. Doing the right thing at the right time means survival. Many of a bird's actions are inborn and it performs them by instinct. But there are important things that a bird must know, which are learned as it grows up. Oddly enough, one of the most important things that many young birds must learn is their own identity. Recognizing their own kind does not always come naturally, strange as it may seem to us.

As with the story of Noah's Ark, people are inclined to sort animals into different kinds, two by two. The animals themselves have been doing this for as long as they have lived in the world. They easily sort themselves out into their different kinds and breed only among themselves. Birds, too, even though many species look very much alike, only rarely make the mistake of trying to court a mate of another species.

Some birds can recognize their own kind naturally. Cuckoos and other parasite birds never really see their parents, yet they know exactly what kind of mate they must select later in life to be able to breed. But many birds go through a critical stage in which they must learn who they are. Whatever they learn at this time is permanent – it cannot be undone afterwards. It is called *imprinting*.

Above: A young duckling clambers over an obstacle to keep up with a life-sized model of its parent. When ducklings hatch, they instinctively follow the parents, who lead them away from the nest to the water. During the first two days of their lives, they "learn" the characteristics of the parent, and become attached to them. If the new-born duckling has to struggle to follow its parents, then the attachment formed is all the stronger for its struggle. Zoologists made young ducklings climb over hurdles to follow a model of their parent. They found that the ducklings that had had to struggle originally were most persistent in trying to follow the model. Forming this attachment is called imprinting. It is a learning process at a critical time in the life of the bird that cannot be undone.

Left: An Eider Duck leads her brood of ducklings to open water. Normally the ducklings become imprinted on their parents and follow them around. A line of ducklings straggling along behind a duck on a lake is a common sight. But if the ducklings are hatched artificially and brought up without their natural parents, they will attach themselves to a foster parent, which may even be a human being. The ducklings will then follow their human "parent" everywhere. When they grow up they will direct all their relationships toward humans instead of ducks! But normal imprinting is valuable to the ducks because it keeps the birds in the company of their own kind.

IMPRINTING

Ducklings and goslings remain in the egg for a long time, and so they are well-developed when they hatch. They have feathers and can walk. One of their first actions is to follow one or both of their parents. The adult birds lead them away from the nest to open water. The instinct to follow is so strong that if the ducklings are deprived of their parents and cared for by others, they will follow any moving object, even a human being!

During these critical few hours, the young bird absorbs the characteristics of the "parent", whether it is a real parent, or a foster parent, such as another bird or a human being. This "parent" becomes representative of what the young bird considers to be its species. When the youngster grows up, it will seek the company of those resembling this "parent" and try to mate with them. This imprinting of an identity cannot be reversed. If the "parent" it follows happens to be a substitute, then the bird will go through life thinking it is some other bird or animal.

In Mallard Ducks, imprinting is strongest when the bird is between 13 and 16 hours old. By 24 hours later, imprinting no longer takes place. If a duckling is forced to accept a strange mother during its first two days of life, it will never learn to live with its own kind. Such mistakes of identity are rare, however since most birds get "imprinted" in terms of their own parents. This method of identification helps in keeping many species of birds distinct and prevents them from breeding with the "wrong" kind. Domestic pigeons come in all colors, but they look for mates that resemble their parents (and therefore resemble themselves). In this way, certain varieties of birds are maintained and do not die out.

Below: Small grassfinches go through a sensitive "imprinting" period when they learn the special features of their own kind. This usually happens when they are between 30 and 40 days old. Bird fanciers often use Bengalese Finches as foster parents to rear young birds of other species. If the young bird is with the Bengalese Finch when it is between 30 and 40 days old, then it will come to think that it is a Bengalese Finch. It will prefer the company of Bengalese Finches, even if it can live with its own kind. If young male Zebra Finches are reared by a female Bengalese Finch (top), they will court female Bengalese Finches when they grow up (bottom). They will do this even if they have an opportunity to mate with female Zebra Finches. Bird fanciers have to be careful about using foster parents, because birds raised in this way will never be able to breed. The 35th day of life is critical for a Zebra Finch if it is to learn which parent is which. When the brood of young finches is between 35 and 40 days old, the male parent chases them away from the home. His hostility at this time seems to teach the young males that they must court females and not males later in life.

A bird is not only imprinted through sight. Wood Ducks nest in holes and the parent bird has to entice the young out of the holes after they hatch. The ducklings become imprinted to the calls of the parent, and later associate with birds that call in the same way. Rails, Moorhens and Coots also become imprinted to calls.

SINGING LESSONS

Singing the song of their particular species does not always come naturally, and many birds literally have to learn to sing. Brood parasites such as the cuckoo develop their song without being taught by others of their own kind, for these birds are "on their own" from the very start of life and do not need imprinting to help gain an identity.

Right: The male White-crowned Sparrow learns its song during the first hundred days of its life, before it can actually sing. It stores up the information it needs by listening to the song of other male White-crowned Sparrows. If it does not hear its fellow males singing at this early stage of its life, the bird will produce an incorrect song later in its life. As the birds learn to sing, differences in song occur between different populations of White-crowned Sparrows. Like human dialects, the farther apart the populations, the more varied are the differences in song.

Below: The male Marsh Warbler (left) and the male Yellow-breasted Chat (right). The ability to copy the phrases of bird song is very important to a bird learning to sing. It is not surprising that some birds should pick up phrases from other different birds in composing their own songs. The Marsh Warbler has been heard to mimic 39 other species of birds. Yellow-breasted Chats are exceptional North American mimics. Together with the Common Jay, the Marsh Warbler is the best mimic in Britain. The best in North America is the Mockingbird.

Many birds, however, need "singing lessons" to learn the proper notes of their song. The young birds will instinctively try to sing, but the results are not very tuneful. They need to hear other birds of their own kind singing before they can sing properly.

Zoologists have studied the songs of chaffinches. Young chaffinches reared by hand and kept from their fellows developed a song that was the correct length and had the correct number of notes, but they did not phrase the song correctly. The young go through two sensitive periods (comparable to imprinting) when they learn the proper details from listening to the song of full grown birds. The first lesson takes place when the young bird is in the nest or has just left it. The second lesson is during the following spring, when it can practice with other chaffinches.

Not all birds learn to sing by imitation. Some birds are merely put into a singing mood by hearing others sing. They do not copy the others, but rely on their own inventiveness. In other cases, the birds are quite inventive if left to their own devices. But when they hear the song of their own kind, they stop trying to devise a song, and learn the proper one.

Most songs seem to be learned from other birds in the same region, and some birds develop local "dialects," just as human beings do. The dialect is handed down to the young birds, who imitate it. Among Crows for example, songs in the local dialect may get a better response from the birds in that region than songs in another dialect.

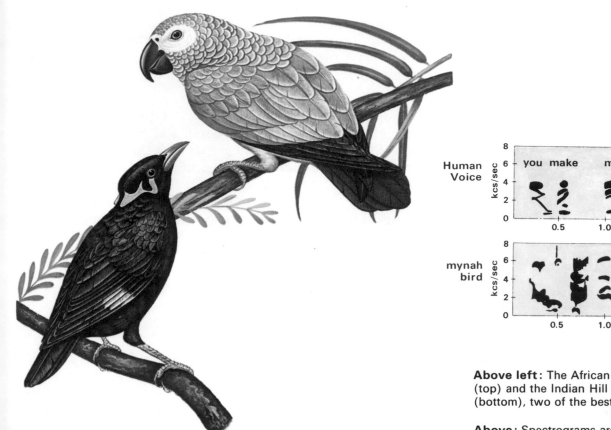

Spectrogram labels:

Human Voice — kcs/sec — you make — me — laugh
0.5 1.0 1.5 2.0

mynah bird — kcs/sec
0.5 1.0 1.5 2.0

Above left: The African Gray Parrot (top) and the Indian Hill Mynah (bottom), two of the best talking birds.

Above: Spectrograms are visual records of bird calls. They show how the pitch of the notes in a call changes. The spectrograms above show the sentence "You make me laugh" as spoken by a human voice and by a mynah bird. The striking similarity of the two indicates that the bird made a remarkable imitation of the human voice. Parrots often learn that certain sounds go with certain events, and they can remember them and mimic them. Parrots have been known to say "Hello" whenever a telephone rings.

Because many birds learn to sing by imitating adult birds, it is not surprising that some of them pick up the songs of other species. The Robin Chat of Africa sometimes produces a song that is made up entirely of phrases borrowed from other birds. The American Mockingbird has been heard to imitate 55 other birds in the space of an hour! In the wild, birds may mimic other birds, or even the cries of preying animals, in order to divert an intruder from its nest, or to frighten it away.

TALKING BIRDS

Some birds are so good at imitation that they can even mimic the human voice. Talking birds such as parrots and mynah birds probably form an attachment to their keepers and pick up their phrases. These birds often "talk" when they are alone, perhaps in an effort to bring their owners to them. They cannot understand the meaning of the words they utter so well. But they do associate sounds with events. A parrot can learn to say "Good-by" when people leave a room. It may then start to say "Good-by" when people that it dislikes are in the room, presumably to try and get rid of them!

MIGRATION

For thousands of years, people have watched birds gather together as the winter or summer approaches and fly off in huge flocks. We may even envy their ability to fly away from a cold winter. If we live in uncomfortably hot climates, we may wish we too could leave for cooler areas.

Entire populations of certain birds will migrate north or south every year. Giant Petrels and many albatrosses that nest on lonely islands in the southern oceans migrate all the way around the world between their breeding seasons, blown by the "roaring forties" and other winds in that hemisphere.

Migration helps birds to survive, since they can "follow" their own good weather. Insect-eaters feast on the hoardes of insects that can be found in the north during the spring and summer. But when winter approaches and the harsh weather brings on a scarcity of food, such birds migrate south to more hospitable regions.

LONG DISTANCE TRAVELERS

Some birds migrate exceptionally long distances. Arctic Terns probably hold the record. They breed every summer as close to the North Pole as the land reaches – about five hundred miles away. Then they migrate down the Atlantic coasts of Europe and Africa to the Antarctic Circle and back every year, making a round trip of nearly 36,000 miles! These birds follow the sun as they migrate from one polar region to the other, and they probably see more daylight during their lives than any other creature in the world.

Other long-distance travelers are the Pacific Golden Plover, which flies non-stop across two thousand miles of ocean twice a year, and the tiny Ruby-throated Hummingbird, which makes a non-stop trip of five hundred to a thousand miles across the Gulf of Mexico.

KEEPING TRACK OF BIRDS

Bird watchers look for flocks of migrating birds every year. They time them, note which birds are taking part in the migration, and watch to see how the weather affects the flocks.

Below: The Slender-billed Shearwater has one of the longest migration routes of any bird. It breeds on the islands in Bass Strait between Tasmania and Australia. Then the birds migrate in a great circle completely around the Pacific Ocean. The journey takes three or four years, and the shearwater usually returns to the island where it was reared to raise its own young.

breeding area
migration route

In many countries, special efforts are made to put marked bands or rings around the birds' legs before they migrate. Anyone seeing a banded bird should try to note the information on the ring and send it back to the central agency in charge of banding with a notation of where and when the bird was seen. In this way, scientists can discover exactly what routes migrating birds follow and how long their journeys take.

Radar has helped to track flocks of birds, just as it helps airport traffic controllers keep a watch on aircraft. It has disclosed that many flocks of migrating birds fly at heights of three thousand feet or more. These high-altitude flights are often different from the low-flying bird movements that bird watchers see from the ground. It is possible that the low-flying birds have become separated from the main high-flying flock. Another advantage of using radar to track birds is that it can be used at night. This is important, for many birds migrate under cover of darkness to escape their enemies.

Satellites orbiting around the earth in space are keeping watch on the migration of large animals such as elk. The animals carry radio transmitters which continuously broadcast their position to the satellite. One day, the transmitters may be made small enough to attach to a bird like a leg band, and then we shall be able to monitor the entire flight of a migrating bird.

FINDING THE WAY

A migratory bird gets "itchy wings" and begins to feel the need to move on as the days get shorter at the end of its breeding season. The shortening days change the balance of hormone chemicals in the bird's body. This change makes the bird feed ravenously. It puts on weight – valuable fat which will give the bird fuel for its long flight. Suddenly it is time to go. The birds assemble in a great wheeling, twittering flock in the sky and fly off toward the warm wintering grounds. It is an amazing sight.

No one really knows exactly how birds are able to fly such vast distances without getting lost. Many birds have a homing ability, and if released a long way from home will find their way back. The homing ability is well developed in migrating birds. One bird was observed to fly home three thousand miles across the Atlantic Ocean in $12\frac{1}{2}$ days. The bird apparently knew exactly where it was going.

Opposite page: The American Golden Plover is one of the world's great travelers. The western race, the Pacific Golden Plover, breeds in the far northern regions of Alaska and Siberia. To migrate, it wings its way non-stop across two thousand miles of the Pacific Ocean to Hawaii. It may then fly on farther south. The eastern race makes an even longer journey. It breeds across northern Canada. As winter approaches, the adult birds migrate to their winter home in South America. They make a 2,300 mile journey over Labrador, Newfoundland and the Atlantic Ocean. The young birds do not attempt the ocean crossing, but fly down the middle of the Continent instead. But all the birds come back overland. The returning plovers use the Mississippi Flyway for part of their route. This extends along the Mississippi River and includes the states that lie along the river. It is one of four fly-ways used by birds in the United States. The Central Flyway lies between Montana and the Dakotas and due south. The Atlantic Flyway and Pacific Flyway lie along the east and west coasts of the country.

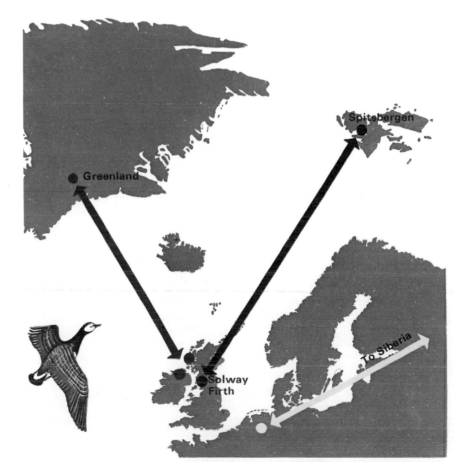

Western race—summer area
Eastern race—summer area
Eastern race—winter area
Flight path of Western race to winter area
Flight path of adult Eastern birds on return journey
Flight path of young Eastern birds on return journey
Flight path of adult Eastern birds on outward journey
Flight path of young Eastern birds on outward journey

Right: Barnacle Geese have various breeding areas. From Holland they go to Siberia, from the Solway Firth in Scotland to Spitsbergen, and from other parts of Scotland and Ireland to Greenland. This information was obtained by banding. Barnacle Geese got their name during the Middle Ages, when people knew nothing of the northern lands in which they bred. It was mistakenly believed that they hatched from certain barnacles that had long stalks like goosenecks.

Spitsbergen

Greenland

To Siberia

Solway
Firth

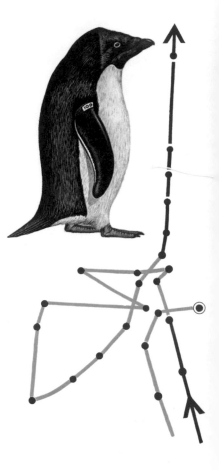

Above: Racing pigeons are able to navigate and find their way home over great distances. The maps show the directions that some birds took on being released from various places up to about 120 miles from their loft. None of the pigeons flew in the opposite direction to the home loft, and most began to fly straight toward it. It is possible that the pigeon may be able to navigate from the position of the sun in the sky. But the pigeon's complete navigation method is probably much more complicated than this.

Left: Most homing birds lose their homing ability if they are taken too far from home. But Manx Shearwaters find their way back over really long distances. Several shearwaters were taken from the island of Skokholm, a bird sanctuary off the coast of Wales. They were released in various parts of Europe, and one was taken across the Atlantic Ocean to Boston. All the birds found their way back to the island in a short time. The bird from Boston took only 12½ days to make its journey of three thousand miles! The bird's speedy return indicated that it must have taken the most direct route!

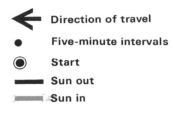

← Direction of travel

● Five-minute intervals

◎ Start

▬▬ Sun out

▬▬ Sun in

Opposite page: An Adélie Penguin, trying to find its way on a field of ice, where everything looks the same, navigates by the sun. The black dots show its position every five minutes. When the sun was out, it moved purposefully over the ice in a straight line (black lines). But when the sun disappeared, it seemed to lose its way and wandered about aimlessly in all directions (blue lines). As soon as the sun reappeared, the penguin set off in a straight line again.

Right: Birds were captured making a stop at a bird sanctuary at Rossiten or Rybachi, near Kaliningrad in Russia, during their spring migration. The birds, young Hooded Crows, were taken 470 miles west to Flensburg in Germany. There they were banded and released. Many of the birds were later recaptured a long way west of their summer homes. They had continued their journey in the direction they would have followed had they been leaving Rossiten after their stopover.

Birds seem to be able to navigate according to the position of the sun and pattern of the stars, and many migrating birds get lost if it is cloudy. Each migrating bird seems to have an inborn ability to fix its position and fly a set course by the sun and the stars. Human navigators also do this, but they need a sextant to observe the position of the sun and stars, and an accurate chronometer to determine the exact time. Birds have an inborn biological clock and seem to know the exact time at any instant. Somehow, they have no need for instruments.

Birds can also alter course if they get blown off-route by side winds. They may estimate the distance that they are drifting off-course by watching landmarks – islands below or cloud formations overhead – or from the direction at which the wind blows against their feathers.

It is possible to fool migrating birds. Zoologists captured some young crows that were halfway through a migration flight to the north. They moved them a long way to the west and released them. Many flew on in the same direction, as if nothing had happened, and so ended up a long way to the west of their breeding grounds. This experiment was also tried with migrating starlings. The young birds were fooled, but the older birds who had migrated before turned up at their usual winter quarters.

Migration and navigation are still great mysteries to us. Much remains to be discovered, not only about how birds navigate, but also about all the other fascinating and complicated actions that we can observe in birds.

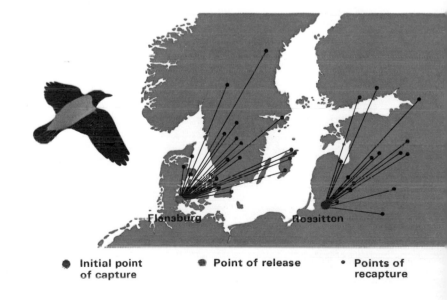

● Initial point of capture   ● Point of release   · Points of recapture

INDEX

Figures in bold type refer to illustrations and captions

Aggression, 30, **34–35**, 35, **39**, **42**, 59, 62, **63**
Alarm calls, 34–35
Albatross, 69
    Royal Albatross, 55
Anting, **13**, **14**
Appeasement behaviour, 35, **35**, **42**
Arena birds, 46–49, **48**, **50**
Attack behaviour, 9, 34
Auk, 59
Avadavat, Red, **15**, **44**, 46, **47**
Avocet, 14
    American Avocet, **32**

Banding, 70, **71**, **73**
Bathing, 10–11, **10–11**
Beak, **8**, 12, 14, **14–15**, 62, **62**
Bill, *see* Beak
Bird of Paradise, 49–50, **50**
Birds of Prey, 21, 22, 28, 34
    see also Eagle, Owl, Vulture
Bittern, 8, 41
Blackbird, **23**, **33**
Black-capped Chickadee, **30**
Blushing, 45, **45**
Bowerbird, 24, 49–51
    Satin Bowerbird, **49**
    Tooth-billed Bowerbird, **50**
Breeding, 7, **7**, 35, 36–63, **36–63**, 69
    see also Courtship
Bullfinch, **15**
Bustard, 13
    Great Bustard, 31, **37**
Buzzard, Red-tailed, 52

Cacique, Yellow-rumped, 59, **59**
Call notes, 34–35
Camouflage, 28, **29**, 55, 59, **63**
Canary, 7, **8**, **52**, 53
Capercaillie, **46**
Cassowary, 13
Chaffinch, **17**, **34**, 37, 67
Cleaning, 10–14, **10–15**
Cock-of-the-Rock, **48**, 49
Cockatoo, Leadbeater's, **46**
Colonies, **28**, 38, 59, 63
Communication, 32–35, **32–35**
Contact species, 29
Coot, 66
Cormorant, 13, **40**, 55
Courtship, 40–51, **40–51**
    dances, **38–39**, 42–44
    feeding, 46, **47**
    postures, **37**, **38**, **40–41**, 41–43, **43**, 46–51
Cowbird, 57–58
Crane, Crowned, **38**
Crossbill, **19**, 21
Crow, 13, 25–26, 67, 73
    Carrion Crow, 38, **58**
    Hooded Crow, **73**
    Pied Crow, 59
Cuckoo, **26**, **57**, 57–58, 64, 66

Black-billed Cuckoo, 58
Common Cuckoo, **56**
European Cuckoo, 57, 58
Yellow-billed Cuckoo, 58

Dawn chorus, 41
Displacement activities, 44
Display, 8, 35, **39**, **42**, 42–49, **44–45**, 60
Dominance, 31
Drinking, 16, **16–17**, 18–19, **31**
Drongos, 11
Duck, 44, 60, **64**, 64–65
    Black-headed Duck, 57
    Eider Duck, 54, 63, **64**
    Mallard Duck, **12**, **40**
    Mandarin Duck, **31**, **42**, 65
    Shelduck, **42**
    Wood Duck, 66
Dust bathing, 11, **12**

Eagle, 17, 18
    Bald Eagle, 18
    Brown Harrier Eagle, **6**
    Golden Eagle, 37
Eating, *see* Feeding
Eggs, 52–58, **54–58**
Egret, Cattle, 27, **27**
Emu, 13
Estrogen, 53
Evolution, 8
Extinct birds, 20, 36

Family protection, 61–63
Feathers, 9, 44, **45**, 45–47
Feeding, 16–27, **16–27**, 30, 31
    partnerships, 26–27
Feeding young, 60, 60–61
Feet, **8**, **22**, 22–23
Fighting, 37; *see also* Aggression
Finch, 13, 17, 38, 52
    Bengalese Finch, **65**
    Crimson Finch, **35**
    Cuban Finch, **13**
    Gouldian Finch, 43
    Melba Finch, **57**
    Parrot Finch, **60**
    Purple Finch, **30**
    Spice Finch, **43**
    Woodpecker Finch, **22**, 23
    Zebra Finch, **35**, 43, 62, **62**, **65**
Flamingo, 16, **18**, 21, 63
Flight, **32**, 33
    calls, 34
    intention movements, **40–41**
Flocks, 28, **29–30**, 31, 33, 69–70
Flycatcher,
    Crested Flycatcher, 54
    Pied Flycatcher, 61
    Tyrant Flycatcher, 59
Flyways, 70
Frogmouth, 13

Gallinule, Purple, **22**
Game birds, 60
Gannet, 55
    Australian Gannet, **34**
    North Atlantic Gannet, **39**
Gardener, 51
    Crestless Gardener, **51**
Goldeneye, **41**
Goldfinch, European, **10**, **47**

Goose, 64–65
    Barnacle Goose, **71**
    White-fronted Goose, **19**
Grassfinch, **17**, **65**
Grebe, Great Crested, **38**, **41**, 42, 44
Greenfinch, **16**, **17**
Grouse, 11
    Black Grouse, **37**
    Sand Grouse, **17**
Guillemot, 54
Gull, 13, **23**, 24, 27, **27**, 59 63
    Black-headed Gull, 38, 58
    Herring Gull, **42**, 58, 61, 62
    Laughing Gull, 18

Hawfinch, **19**
Hawk, 17
    Redtailed Hawk, 59
Heron, 14, 20, 22, 44, 59
    Gray Heron, **41**
    Green Heron, 24
    Night Heron, 62, **63**
Homing, 70
Honeycreeper, Hawaiian, **18**
Honey Guide, **26**, 27, 57–58
Hoopoe, 14
Hormones, 36, 53, 70
Hornbill, 11, **47**, 55
    Great Hornbill, 13
Huia, **21**
Hummingbird, 14, 16, 17, 19, 20, 51
    Puff-legs Hummingbird, **18**
    Ruby-throated Hummingbird, 69

Imprinting, 64–67, **64–65**
Incubation, 55–57, **56**
Inheritance, 9
Injury feigning, 63
Instinct, 9, 19, **23**, 24, 58, **60**, 61, 64, 67
Intelligence, 24–25

Jay,
    Blue Jay, **30**
    Common Jay, **13**, **35**, **67**
    European Jay, **16**, 26
    Gray Jay, **24**
Junco,
    Arizona Junco, **66**
    Oregon Junco, **66**

Kingfisher, **11**, 20
    Common Kingfisher, **21**
Kiskadee, 59
Kite, Everglade, **21**
Kittiwake, **58**

Lammergeyer, **23**, 24
Language, 32, 41
Lark, 11
    Horned Lark, 61
    Skylark, **29**
Learning, 9, 19, **22**, 24, **34**, 64–68
Leks, **37**, 47–49, **48**
Linnet, **17**
Lovebird, 61
    Black-masked Lovebird, **43**
    Madagascar Lovebird, **43**
Lyre Bird, **48**, 49

Macaw, Hyacinth, **14**
Maleo Fowl, 56
Mallard, *see* Duck
Mallee Fowl, **55**, 56
Manakin, 52
   Bronze-winged Manakin, **10**
Markings, **32**, 33
Martin, 60
Meadow Pipit, 57, **57**
Megapode, 54, 55—56
Merganser,
   Hooded Merganser, **40**, **41**
   Red-breasted Merganser, **20**, 21
Migration, 34, 69—73, **69—73**
Mimicry, 68
Mobbing, 63
   calls, 34
Mockingbird, **7**, **67**, 68
Moorhen, 66
Mynah Bird, 7, 68
   Indian Hill Mynah Bird, **68**

Natural selection, 8
Navigation, 73, **73**
Nest building, 52—54, **52—54**
Nesting, 52—60, **52—63**
Nesting sites, 9, 38, 40, 60, 63
Nightingale, 7, **33**
Nightjar, **19**, **33**
Nutcracker, Thick-billed, **25**
Nuthatch, European, 24

Oiling, 12—13, **12**, **15**
Oriental White-eye, **12**
Oriole, Black-throated, 52
Osprey, 18
Ostrich, 13, 23, **23**
Owl, 17, 22
   Snowy Owl, 59
   Tawny Owl, **6**
Oxpecker, 27
Oystercatcher, European, 14, 20, **32**, **34**, 38

Parasite birds, 57—58, 64, 66
Parrot, 7, 11, 14, 21, 22, 68
   African Gray Parrot, **68**
Peacock, 43, **45**, 45—46
Pecking order, **30**, 31
Pelican, 20
   Brown Pelican, 18, **21**
Penguin, 13, 18, 63
   Adélie Penguin, **44**, **73**
   Emperor Penguin, 29, 53, **56**
   King Penguin, **53**, **56**
   Yellow-eyed Penguin, **36**
Petrel, Giant, 69
Pheasant, 11
   Argus Pheasant, **45**, 46
   Golden Pheasant, 45
   Ring-necked Pheasant, **36**
Pigeon, **7**, 18, 60, 65
   Bluecrowned Pigeon, **46**
   Passenger Pigeon, 36
   Racing Pigeon, **72**
   Wood Pigeon, 16
Plover, Golden, 63, 69, **70**
Plumage, 12—14, 41, 49
Postures, 9, 32
Powder down, 14
Prairie Chicken, Greater, 47
Preening, **11**, 12—14, **12**, **13**, **15**
   Social preening, **12**, 13, **34**
Protective associations, 59—60, **59**

Ptarmigan, 27
   Rock Ptarmigan, 28

Rail, 66
Rearing young, **36**, 38, 57—63, **58—63**
Reproduction, *see* Breeding
Ring Dove, **17**
Ring Ouzel, **33**
Ringing, *see* Banding
Rituals, 9, **31**, **42**, 43, **45**
Robin,
   American Robin, 9, **60**
   European Robin, 9, 10, 19, **26**, 27, 37, **60**, **63**
Robin Chat, 68
Ruff, 47, **48**
Ruffling, 13, 43

Sandpiper, Purple 63
Scratching, 14, **14**, **43**
Sea birds, 17, 38
   see also Gull
Seeds, **19**, 21
Shearwater,
   Manx Shearwater, **72**
   Slender-billed Shearwater, **69**
Shelduck, *see* Duck
Shrike, 25, 28
Singing, *see* Songs
Skimmer, **18**, 21
Skua, 63
Skylark, *see* Lark
Snipe, Painted, 37
Social birds, 30
   see also Colonies, Flocks, Pecking Order
Songbirds, **7**
Songs, **33**, 34, **34**, 35, 40, 66—67
Sparrow, 10, 19, 57, 60
   House Sparrow, **12**
   Song Sparrow, **66**
   White-crowned Sparrow, **66**
Species, 6
Spectrograms, **68**
Spoonbill, 19
Stamping, 22
Starling, **14**, 28, **28**, **30**, 60, 73
Stilt, 14
Storing food, **24**, **25**, 25—26
Stork,
   Marabou Stork, 59
   White Stork, 60
Sunbirds, 17
Survival, 7, 8, 10, 33, 58, **58**, 69
Swallow, 9, 54, 60
   Barn Swallow, 52
Swan, Mute, **40**
Swift, 14, 29, 60
Swiftlet, 54

Tailor Bird, **53**
Talking birds, 68
Tanager, 59
Tern, **11**, 13, 63
   Arctic Tern, **61**, 69
   Sandwich Tern, **35**
Territory, 9, **34**, 37—41
Thrush, Song, **11**, 19, 23, 24
Titmouse **8**, 16, 22, 26, 29, 34
   Blue Titmouse, 21
   Great Titmouse, **8**
Tool using **22—23**, 23—24, 51

Toucan, 19
Tree Creeper, 29
Turaco, 14
Turkey, 11, 45, **45**

Vireo, 52
Vitamin D, 13
Vulture, 18, 22
   Bearded Vulture, **23**
   Egyptian Vulture, 23, **23**

Wading birds, 22
Warbler,
   Black-throated Warbler, 59
   Marsh Warbler, **67**
   Reed Warbler, **57**
   Savi's Warbler, **33**
   Wood Warbler, 14
Water Birds, 11, 17, 20; *see also* Duck
Waxbill, 61
   Violet-eared Waxbill, **58**
Waxwing, Bohemian, **30**
Weaverbird, **52**, 57, 59, 60
   Social Weaver, **53**, 54
   Viduine Weaver, 57
   Village Weaver, **54**
Whitethroat, **55**
Whydah, **57**
   Paradise Whydah, **57**
   Pin-tailed Whydah, **58**
Willet, **32**
Woodpecker, 20
   Acorn Woodpecker, 25
   Great Spotted Wood-pecker, **20**, 24
Wren, 29

Yellow-breasted Chat, **67**